HE WHO BELIEVES IN ME
WILL NEVER DIE
JESUS
THE LIGHT OF THE WORLD

DIVINE INSPIRATIONS

THE IMMACULATE CONCEPTION AND THE SACRED HEART OF JESUS
UNITE THE WORLD

HE WHO BELIEVES IN ME WILL NEVER DIE
JESUS
THE LIGHT OF THE WORLD

Divine Inspirations from Jesus and Mary for Love of Many

through Geraldine

First American Edition

1999

NIHIL OBSTAT:

Reverend Marco Chiolerio, OCD

IMPRIMATUR:

The Most Reverend Jaroslav Škarvada
Vicar General and Consecrating Bishop
Archdiocese of Prague
Czech Republic

12 January 1996

An Imprimatur is an official declaration
that a book or pamphlet is free of doctrinal or moral error.

First American Edition
Typeset in the Czech Republic
by ArchArt, P. O. Box 14, Praha 9

Published
by Queenship Publishing Company
Goleta, California 93116
United States of America
1999

Cost:

This book is not for sale. It is distributed free. However, voluntary offerings will be
gratefully accepted to defray the considerable cost of printing and distribution
(and keeping in mind poorer people who cannot afford donations).
Also there are other messages to be published. The printing of these will be made possible
through the help received.

The distribution centres are listed in Appendix G, page 204. Contact one of these centres for a copy of the book. Contributions towards the cost of publication of the book may be given to any one of these Distribution Centres.

ISBN 1-57918-116-3 (PB)
ISBN 1-57918-117-1 (HB)

Acknowledgements

Special thanks to friends, without whose help this publication would not have been possible, and to Father Richard Masin, now in Russia, who has been a zealous worker and inspiration for the publication of this book.

"To my Mum, for her support and encouragement. I would also like to give heartfelt thanks to my Grandmother, because she prayed that we might all lead good lives and I feel God touched my life through her prayers.

'Mother' (Geraldine's Grandmother now deceased, who had a big part in raising her), *until we are together again, this is my gift to you."*

Geraldine

With gratitude we acknowledge the Hampton Marian Centre for the use of the Two Hearts picture. These pictures are available at: Hampton Marian Centre, 261 Hampton Street, Victoria 3188, Australia (Catalogue No. 2H2).

We acknowledge with thanks permission for the use of the Divine Mercy image reproduced on the back cover of this book, the copyright of Divine Mercy Publications Ltd., Ireland, who make the message of Divine Mercy available in English, as revealed to Blessed Faustina. For further information write to Divine Mercy Publications, Maryville, Co. Dublin, Ireland.

With deep gratitude we also acknowledge the contribution of Pavol Cesnak of Bratislava, Slovakia, who drew the pictures of Jesus and Mary for us used on the pages.

Foreword

BISHOP G. F. MAYNE A.M., D.D.
CATHOLIC MILITARY ORDINARY
30 WHITE CRESCENT
P.O. Box 63 CAMPBELL, A.C.T. 2601
AUSTRALIA. TEL (06) 248 0257, 248 0511

23.1.'96.

The message contained in these private revelations is deserving of prayerful reflection and meditation. I can see no reason why they should not be published.

May this publication help all readers to truly appreciate the infinite love of the Sacred Heart of Jesus and the Immaculate Heart of Mary for every human being.

Divine Mercy is always available to those who, with true repentance and humility turn to the loving Father,

+ Geoffrey F. Mayne

ADVENIAT REGNUM TUUM

Fax No. (06) 247 0898

Introduction by former Spiritual Director

✝ РИМСКО-КАТОЛИЧЕСКОЕ ОБЪЕДИНЕНИЕ

ПРИХОД ПРЕОБРАЖЕНИЯ ГОСПОДА

Tver, Russia
Feast of the Immaculate Conception
8 December, 1994

Dear Friend,

This little book can be your ladder to Heaven. It comes from a Mother and Her Son, pleading with Her children to return to God, the Father. A Mother and Her Son weeping tears of anguish for a humanity that has lost its way, that cannot tell its left hand from its right.

The call to conversion is simple: goodwill, prayer, penance, and leading a Sacramental life that is pleasing to God.

A journey of a thousand miles starts with a step. May this little book be your help and your guide to that first, small, but oh, so important step.

To the greater glory of God,
in the most Holy Trinity.

Richard H. Masin

Father Richard H. Masin
Parish Priest, Tver (formerly Kalinin)
Russia

My treasure of treasures for this time

29 August 1996

Jesus:

"My beloved daughter, it is I, Jesus, your beloved Saviour. Daughter of My Most Sacred Heart, I wish you to give My Priest representatives this message concerning this treasure of treasures, 'Divine Inspirations'.

I, Jesus, desire this book to be two inches bigger and one inch wider.* I desire all who read this book to have great reverence for what is contained therein. This treasure is from My Sacred Heart and is to be taken seriously by all.

I do not desire two sizes, as I requested one book from the beginning to meet the requirements of all. I also wish the print to be large and of fine quality as this is My treasure of treasures for this time. You may request hard and soft copies.

Know that all who have worked or helped and prayed for this work will participate in the glory of the Most Holy Trinity, because of all who are converted and brought closer to My Sacred Heart.

Beloved holy ones, the Evil One is trying to destroy My precious work now, do not be discouraged, I, Jesus, am with you all.

Go forward, My mighty ones, into battle, for all of My Kingdom are rejoicing at the approaching birth of 'Divine Inspirations' and of My abundant Mercy to be reproclaimed again as My greatest gift to mankind
in these very evil times.
Go in peace."

* *Two sizes for printing had already been chosen.*

May all who gaze on these pictures receive special graces

29 August 1996

Jesus:

"Beloved daughter, it is My desire that the picture of Divine Mercy be full page to promote devotion to My Divine Mercy, and the picture of My Holy Mother's Heart and Mine be of a decent size to also draw attention to Our Hearts which are joined together as one.

So the size I have given you is to be added to the large book size.

This I desire so that all attention may be drawn to these special devotions, given for these wicked times in which you live.

May all who gaze on these pictures receive special graces from Our Hearts and from the Holy Trinity in whom great love is given to these devotions."

Dedication

The dedication and prayer is at Jesus' request (24 August 1994)

"This book is dedicated to the Holy Family of Jesus,
Mary and Joseph.

Prayer

Father, bless all who read this book
and may all hearts be opened to receive
the graces contained therein.
I ask this in the name of Jesus,
through the intercession of Mary and Joseph.

Amen."

Introduction by the Spiritual Director

In the course of a telephone conversation, Geraldine, the recipient of these messages first told me of the experience of God which had changed her life. Geraldine is a wife and the mother of a young family. Her surname is being withheld so that her home life may be protected. Through the experience just mentioned Geraldine had resumed the practice of her Catholic faith and has become as close to a daily communicant as she can manage.

At the time when she first spoke to me of her experiences her Spiritual Director was Fr. Michael Love SJ. She also had a previous Spiritual Director Fr. Richard Masin who had gone to Czechoslovakia (before the division into the Czech and Slovak Republics) and is now in Russia.

In the latter half of 1993, Fr. Love became ill and was diagnosed as having cancer. As Geraldine began asking advice from me more often I asked Fr. Love as to whether he believed in the genuineness of the messages. He was definite in his answer that he did.

I too, observed that the signs of genuineness seemed to be present. The messages and the life Geraldine was trying to lead were good and in harmony with the teaching of the Church. There was no personal advantage involved for her, rather a deal of suffering. She appeared to me to be a balanced person.

The fruits of the experiences and messages in Geraldine's life were prayer, frequent reception of the Sacraments, Eucharistic Adoration, greater harmony in the family, zeal to spread prayer groups, prayer and care for individuals, sometimes receiving messages for individuals who were generally greatly helped by them. Also Geraldine is a very caring and charitable person. The fruits for others were that people were encouraged to pray more, to pray in groups, to persevere in Christian ideals, challenged to live better lives and to find joy and consolation in the love of God, Mary and the Saints.

In the course of the messages, Jesus and Mary requested that the messages be compiled into a book and that this would be published to help as many as possible.

The best way to read the messages that follow is to read a message, then pause and reflect. May everyone, who reads these messages prayerfully, come closer through them to God, to Our Blessed Lady, to the Saints, Angels and the Holy Souls.

Father Eugene Szondi (Spiritual Director)

The Medal

Early June 1994

"Daughter, it is I, Holy Mother, please write for souls. My child, you must tell Father I desire and My Divine Son, Jesus also requires, the messages regarding the medal to be placed at the front of the book in an appropriate place, all this on one page. My child, My beloved Son, Jesus, and I desire a medal to be struck. I wish this medal to be spread far and wide as this is the Medal of Divine Mercy and of devotion to Our Two Hearts. Let all who spread devotion to our Two Hearts and Divine Mercy be assured of a very special place in Heaven. These devotions rekindled will be the onset to the triumph of My Immaculate Heart, which My Son desires greatly. Pray much for this intention and for these last days preceding the triumph of My Immaculate Heart.

My beloved child, may the greatest blessing of Almighty God be upon all who do as I ask. Go in peace."

This is the description which Our Lady gave of the medal:

The front of medal:

The Two Hearts
with the inscription

"The Immaculate
Conception
and the Sacred Heart
of Jesus unite the World"

The back of medal:

Jesus of Mercy
with the inscription

"Jesus the Light
of the World.
He who believes in Me
will never die."

Our Lady:

"I will personally bless anyone who wears this medal, it is a sign of My love."

Other messages relating to the medal:

14 June 1994 *Tuesday*

Holy Mother:

"I have appeared to you under the title of:

**'MOTHER OF THE WORLD,
CONSOLER OF HEARTS'.**

I have come to give you My peace and love and to bring My children closer to Our TWO HEARTS."

10 February 1995 *Friday* *St. Scholastica Memorial*

Holy Mother:

"My child, this medal will be for the conversion of many. Many graces and blessings, healings and spiritual healings will come from the faith people have in this devotion. The name of this medal, My child, is 'the Medal of Divine Mercy'. I have come to ask for devotion to Our Two Hearts and to My Beloved Son's Divine Mercy. Those who seek Us under these titles will receive abundant blessings, and the grace of My Son will be given them. This devotion will spread worldwide and will amaze you. It is the will and work of My Divine Son, so it will bear much fruit. Go, My children, and spread this devotion everywhere as it is so necessary for the salvation of the world. My Son blesses you as do I. Go in peace."

14 February 1995 *Monday* *Sts. Cyril and Methodius Memorial*

Sister Faustina:

"My beloved sister in Christ, I am happy you desire to speak with me. Jesus, our beloved Master, wishes to use you as He did others to bring devotion to His Divine Mercy. My prayers will be very much with you and I am to help and

intercede for you, so that in times of great trial you will have help and assistance. This medal is of great significance and brings great joy to my heart. Wear it with great love and sacrifice everything on behalf of this devotion. Many, my sister, will ask for this medal, it will be much sought after, so pray and never lose hope or despair as many souls depend on your sacrifices for their salvation. I will be with you always to help, guide and comfort you in great and difficult moments, but remember, never lose heart because your reward is never-ending. Sister, I give you my love and my special sisterly blessing on this medal. Amen."

(This message was given while I was praying in front of the Blessed Sacrament after Mass and Rosary.)

Contents

1992

1993

1976

1.

Never be afraid to pray

The first time I believe I heard Our Lady speak to me was just after the death of my sister Karen, who died at the age of twelve. I was then thirteen and I was having great difficulty dealing with her death, as I had prayed and pleaded with God to spare her. I even promised my life to Him if He would only let her live. However, after years of great, great suffering she died, and I could not forgive God. I was very angry and somehow I blamed myself for her death, and I could not understand why God had taken her and not me, as I would have gladly given my life for hers, because I believed she was a much better person than I was. She had so much more to give than I, she was so loving and kind, gentle and good. I did not consider myself worthy to live, I found myself asking, *"Why didn't You take me instead, Karen was much better than me?"* I used to punish myself a lot and cried endlessly as I hated myself and I could not bear the pain of our separation.

Then one day as I lay on my "mother's" (grandmother's) bed crying with my heart as though it was breaking, I heard a beautiful woman's voice, it was soft, loving and gentle, yet very clear and distinct, **"Stop punishing yourself, it is not your fault."** I jumped with fright as I had thought that I was alone in the room. I looked up and expected to see my grandmother, but to my surprise there was no one there. I was puzzled, but yet I felt calm and peaceful as this voice had somehow comforted and soothed my pain, and from that moment on I did stop punishing myself.

Now at this point in time I was wanting to pray for help, but having blamed God and turned against Him, I now found it very difficult to pray. I could not sleep, I hardly ate and every time I tried to pray I would always get pictures in my mind and nightmares that frightened me greatly. Now I felt I was losing my mind as I had horrible visions of my sister and I was frightened to be alone. All of this took a great toll on my grandmother as she tried to understand what I was going through.

Then one night I had a dream that I was with a group of people going to Lourdes, when suddenly I am lost and on my own in what appeared to be a misty moorland at night time yet I can see a grotto at the top of the hill in the distance, so I make my way

there just as some people are coming out. It looked like a cave and on the inside I see a statue of Our Lady and a kneeler in front of it. I kneel down to ask Our Lady to help me to pray and as I tried to pray, something is pulling at my left arm to distract me, but being so desperate for help I decided to persevere in prayer. I felt a sharp pain in my arm as though something had bitten me. I turned around to see what it was and I saw a huge, black dog. So I cried out to Our Lady, *"Help me please, I can't pray!"* As I look up at the statue, it's gone. There is nothing there. Then I look to my right hand side and this beautiful lady was standing beside me. This statue had come to life. She looked about eighteen and she radiated calmness, serenity and peacefulness, and she was so beautiful. It was as if the word "fear" did not exist for Her. Then She held out Her arms very gracefully and looked at the dog, saying full of love, **"Come dance with Me, Satan!"** At that, this huge dog spun around backwards so fast it drilled a huge hole in the concrete ground and down it went underground in a puff of smoke. I could see this dog was terrified of this woman and hated Her. Then She took me by the hand and walked outside with me. Then She said, **"Geraldine, never be afraid to pray, good always overcomes evil."** I felt Her Motherly love and affection for me, She was so full of motherly love and concern for me.

The next morning this dream stood out in my mind and it seemed very real. As I was sitting at a small table having breakfast with my grandmother I told her about it. To my great surprise my "mother" (grandmother) got down on her knees very excitedly, she kept blessing herself repeatedly saying, "Oh, sweet Jesus! The Blessed Virgin Mary has appeared to you." She kept blessing herself and repeating this, she was giving thanks to God. However, I did not believe this, I just kept trying to get her off the floor, as it was the middle of winter with snow on the ground and because we had not yet finished our extension, and had only a concrete floor and my poor "mother" had bad arthritis, heart trouble, hardly any sight in one eye, and I was worried she would become more sick. So I said, "Mother, it's only a dream," but she believed otherwise.

However, many years later, even though I had never been to Lourdes or seen pictures, I was looking through a book and in it there was a picture of the grotto of Lourdes in which Our Lady had appeared to St. Bernadette and it was the same as the grotto

I had seen in my dream. I was overcome as I realized long after my "mother's" death, that she was right.

1979

2.

Go quickly and make up

In a dream I saw my sister who had died and she was dressed in black. I ran to her to hug and kiss her as I was so happy to see her, when I noticed she was upset with me because my grandfather and I had a disagreement over something and we had not resolved it. Then my sister said, "Go quickly and make it up with him." She was upset with me because I was being selfish and unkind, so the next morning I told my Mum* and she said to go and do this.** I said I would go in the morning (the next day). That night my grandmother woke us up saying he had died of a heart attack, now I realized why my sister appeared all in black; she came to warn me and to prepare me.

1980

3.

Warning about future events

January 1980

I had a dream, I was driving along in my car, when suddenly I turned and saw my grandfather next to me. He had died one year previously. He wanted desperately to tell me something. He was talking about something that is going to happen to the world. "Pray, pray," he said, "something terrible is going to happen to the world." I laughed, thinking this was not serious. Then he became extremely angry. "Listen!!" he shouted. Instantly upon seeing his seriousness, I knew he wasn't joking. This dream left a big impression on me.

---

* *"Mum", i. e. my mother, not my grandmother.*

** *I. e. make up with him.*

4.
Warning

March 1980

I had a dream that upset me. In it something terrible was happening all around me. People were running and screaming in terror – people are dropping at my feet, dying. I am running in fear too and I barely manage to survive and my family too. I felt this was the end of the world. I am not sure.

After my grandfather's death, he warns me in dreams to prepare for terrible times ahead.

1980–1989

5.
The years between 1980 and 1989

During the next few years I married and had three children. At this period in my life I had drifted away from my faith; I was lucky if I went to Mass once a year at Christmas and I would only pray if I needed something, but when I received it I would forget to say "Thank you".

Then one day my husband asked me if I would go with him to live in Australia. At that time I had all I needed and I did not want to go. Nevertheless I said to God, "If there is a better life than this, then let it happen." So, soon after we emigrated to Australia.

The first few years were very difficult trying to adjust to a new life. I suffered much at this time. It was shortly after this at the birth of my fourth child that I had an experience that greatly changed my life.

Now as I look back over these years I praise and thank God for what He has done in my life. I feel that God has more than made up for all that I have left behind by sending the most wonderful people into my life. Thank You, Jesus!

At first I wrote some messages just for my personal use and because a Religious Sister had encouraged me to do so. From the time I met Father Masin and he became my Spiritual Director,

he insisted that I should write down all the messages and experiences. This was difficult for me because of arthritic pain in my wrist and because many of the messages and experiences were hard to put into words. But as my Spiritual Director wanted it I believed it was the will of God that I should write.

6.

This first experience greatly changed my life

In 1986, I was expecting my fourth child. When I first became pregnant my husband and I were very upset as we already had three children in a row. Thoughts were going through my mind about if I should have this child or not.

While I was feeling this way over my pregnancy, I had a dream in which I had an axe in my hands and I was about to put this axe through a baby's head, and as I looked down, the baby looked up at me and smiled. At that moment, as if I had suddenly awakened, I saw the reality of what I had been thinking of doing and I was horrified. In reality, the dream showed me I was about to murder the child. I realized the evil that was behind my thinking. So from that moment on I asked God to help me through, because my husband and I were finding it very difficult to cope with our present situation. So Divine Help was needed.

The next nine months were terribly hard. I suffered from start to finish, I was in great pain, burning pain all over. When I could bear it no longer, I went to a doctor only to be told I had rheumatoid arthritis. Because I was pregnant, I could not take anything for the pain. So I used to feel like killing myself. Then at five months I had an accident and fractured my spine. I could not walk for two months and lay on my back in hospital for weeks receiving physiotherapy. During this time we knew no one in Australia as all my family were overseas, so I had no help apart from my husband, and all my children were under six. This time was a testing time, a period of great darkness and suffering. I often felt terrible loneliness and I longed for my "mother" (grandmother).

I was told at the hospital that towards the end of my pregnancy I would be in a lot more pain than normal and this proved to be true. It got to the stage that once more I could not walk because my back had given in, so I went into hospital again for a few weeks. When the doctors thought that the baby had grown sufficiently, they induced me and I was in labour for three days. I was on a heart machine, the baby had wires on its head inside me to monitor its heartbeat. My back felt as though it had broken in half. Every time they put a drip in my hand or arm, back or front, it would swell up greatly. After numerous doctors examined me they sent for a specialist. He told me I was in bad health and I was not responding to treatment and that I was suffering from exhaustion. So if the baby did not arrive by evening they would do a Caesarean. He put something strong in the drip again to make the womb contract. This time I knew I was close.

Up until now the hospital staff had been very supportive of me as I watched women come and go, having their babies. Now the change in shifts brought someone new, of whom, from the moment we met, I knew that I would be given a very difficult time. This person saw all the bruising and swelling in my arms and all the machines and wires coming from me and upon realizing the drip was inserted wrongly, pulled it from my arm. The needle broke, half was in my arm and the other half out. I screamed in agony and this person shouted back into my face that it was not her fault. At this point I felt I was at the mercy of someone very ruthless and I was afraid to complain and kept all inside hoping not to aggravate the situation. I had arranged to have a special drug because of the fracture in my spine. Having told this member of staff, she said it was too soon for the drug. Then I was informed I was too far along to be given anything to relieve the pain. I was taken into the delivery suite; normally with pregnancies they lift you from your bed onto a trolley bed, this nurse put me in a wheelchair. At that moment I felt as though my back had been chopped in half. I really felt like the crucified Lord, or I could relate in some way to His suffering. Then I was left in the delivery room with my husband and I felt the baby move down. I felt the baby's head press on the fracture and the pain was too much for me to bear. It was like the births of all the other children put together. I was convinced I would die. In desperation I offered up my pain and gave it to Jesus (I might

add, I had brought the Bible into hospital with me to comfort me and to help me to pray). Then all of a sudden one moment I am lying there in agony and the next I am in a completely different place, standing up free from all pain. I did not know where I was; I looked all around me and everything was brilliant light. In front of me to my left I saw the figure of a man and it was as though the sun was shining from His face, but yet it did not hurt my eyes to look at Him. He was brighter than the sun. At that moment I felt His great compassion for me, as if He felt sorry for me (it reminded me of a brother who loves you very much and wants to help) and then He said, **"Do not worry, this person belongs to the Wicked One."** I knew He meant the nurse who had caused me to suffer much.

Up until this moment in my life, I sometimes wondered if God or Heaven really existed. Now in Jesus' presence I was in awe and remembered thinking, "Oh, my God, there really is a Supreme Being who watches over the whole earth and sees everything." Now I know for sure that there is a God! Then He said: **"They are persecuting My people,** (innocent people who are victims of the wicked)" and He raised His right hand as He wanted to punish the wicked people here on earth. I then felt tremendous anger coming from Him and also I felt His Almighty Power and just as He was about to strike, something from my right hand side stopped Him. I look across to see what it was and I saw a Lady sitting down. (He was standing and She was sitting.) Coming from this Woman were oceans and oceans of love. So much love, a love I have never known. All the love I have for my family, children, husband, mother, grandparents, relatives, everyone, all this love put together is only a tear-drop compared to the love coming from this Lady and a serenity, peacefulness and gentleness on the same scale. Her Love was stopping this Man from punishing the world and I knew I must go through this Lady to get to this Man. She had a tremendous hold over Him, which was Love. In this love that I felt coming from Her I experienced the greatest ecstasy and happiness I had ever known. Then I realized He could refuse Her nothing. At this moment She said to me: **"You are going to have a baby girl. Go back, they need you."** Then I heard my husband calling my name: "Geraldine." I looked down and saw my husband and the nurse in the delivery room. From where I was, I felt like I was looking into Hell, because the difference between where I was

and the earth was so great. Somehow, I could see different degrees of wickedness in people. I could see either their soul or their heart, which, I am not sure. I could see inside of them, something, like I suppose, as God sees them (from here on Geraldine seems to have this gift of insight into peoples' hearts on occasions, that is, whenever God chooses to give it). As my husband's voice got louder, I felt myself being pulled back down towards him. As I realized this I begged, cried and pleaded, "Please don't send me back, please don't send me back, I want to stay." But I was pulled back begging and pleading. I did not want to come back even to my children for whom I would give my life. What a wonderful place this must be, that the love for all my children, whom I love more than life itself, was not enough to bring me back. Jesus says that there is no greater love than to lay down your life for someone. Yet this love was not enough to bring me back as this place was so beautiful, that not only would you suffer anything to get there, but you would gladly beg for more. So I longed to let others know of the most wonderful, wonderful joy that awaits them in Paradise. We only suffer for a short time in this life, but the joy and happiness that awaits us in Heaven is for all eternity.

A moment or two later the baby was born and it was a little girl so I called her "Mary". From this moment on my life changed greatly. Now I knew God was real and Heaven existed and I wanted to go there more than anything. After this I knew that suffering was the greatest gift I could give Jesus (in the sense that suffering united to Christ has an immense value in the eyes of God and obtains many blessings for the world, and great reward in Heaven). I also knew how the Heart of Jesus is wounded and terribly offended when we take His Holy Name in vain. In the next world He is worshipped and adored. He is King of the Universe and His Holy Name is sacred. After this experience I have had great peace and joy. Since then I believe Our Lady and Jesus have been gradually teaching me. One of the great changes was a continual awareness of Jesus' presence with me everywhere; this presence was more real to me than the people actually with me in the same room. I talked to Him about everything and invited Him into every situation. This great awareness lasted for well over a year, then gradually faded, but by then I had grown in my faith.

7.

"I am your Blessed Mother, I am speaking to you."

(The beginning of inner locutions)

November 1989 (At home)

I was feeling very sad this night. It was a week before we went to Medjugorje for the first time, the third anniversary of the experience I had of Jesus and Mary at the birth of my fourth child. Our flight had been cancelled and many things began to go wrong. It was a very stressful time. Then a friend who was also going rang; she said that she had just spoken to her mother and felt so much better. I was happy for her but I also needed my "mother" too (grandmother who had partly raised me and to whom I was very close), and was missing her very much, as I needed advice and I was still grieving for her (she had died in 1982). Then I was thinking with tears streaming down my face of how we used to talk, and of her loving ways, my heart was breaking as I wished she was still here.

Then to my surprise I heard a woman's voice speaking inside of me very clearly; She said, **"I am your Blessed Mother. I am speaking to you from within. Your earthly mother is not here with you right now so I have come to comfort you during your trials. However, your other 'mother'** (grandmother) **is here with Me. Would you like to speak to her?"** At that moment I thought I was losing my mind for willing this to happen. But yet, in spite of my thoughts I felt peaceful and calm and very comforted and loved by this voice. So I said, *"Yes, I would."*

The next thing I knew, somehow, I was flying in spirit through the sky. By my left side was an Angel guiding me and I felt it was my Guardian Angel, and it was night time. Then after some time I saw in the distance a city. As we approached this city, it was like a warm and peaceful Sunday afternoon. I say a Sunday because there was a holiness about it. I saw white stone houses with flat roofs and park bench seats outside. There were people sitting on the seats. As we got closer, I recognized some of the people. My grandmother was sitting on the right side and my

sister, Karen, opposite her. My grandmother looked younger and there was a beautiful glow about her. I could see she was very happy; and also happy to see me. She said that it was not my time yet (as I would have liked to have stayed with her), she said she was very proud of what I was trying to do (i. e. trying to lead a good life), and said she was looking forward to my being with her. She also told me never to forget all that she had taught me. (I understood that it was very important not to forget the good Christian upbringing she gave me.*)

Then I found myself looking towards my sister. It was like looking through a camera as the focus moved from place to place. My sister looked about thirty years old, now a grown woman (she was twelve years old when she died), but her features were the same. She was beaming and so happy and was smiling and she said, "I have someone very, very special here who is really looking forward to meeting you. Don't worry, I am looking after her for you." At that moment the camera went down and she was holding the hand of a little girl about nine years old, with long hair tied back in a ponytail and she wore a plain grey dress. I didn't know who she was.

Then my sister said, "This is Geraldine Margaret." At that moment I nearly fainted with shock. I felt my hair stand up on the back of my head and I felt hot, then cold, as I realized it was the little baby I had miscarried nine years earlier and it was a girl. I was going to call her Margaret Geraldine after my grandmother, but instead they called her after me. Then this experience ended and as I came out of the room, my husband said, "What's the matter?" as he could see by the look on my face something had happened, so I related to him my experience.

Then I cried continuously at the thought of having a daughter and not knowing her. Again I was so upset not knowing what to make of all this, when again I heard this beautiful soft loving woman's voice. **"Do not be sad at what you have seen. Rejoice, rejoice for your Father in Heaven has given you a wonderful gift."** Again I stopped crying and was comforted and felt great peace. Her words seem to put a balm on my sorrow and hurts. From this time on I heard this beautiful voice many times,

* *I. e. always to love and respect my mother, that is to keep the Commandment of honouring father and mother, to overlook any faults or hurts, just to offer it up to God and never to bear grudges. She taught me that God would bless me for this.*

comforting me, consoling me, teaching me, guiding me, correcting me and preparing me for what is to come. When I think back over my life at the most difficult times I would hear this comforting voice but I never thought anything of it. But yet I was always surprised when things would come true. But now this voice and presence is constant and more prominent in my life so much so I cannot imagine life without it.

1990

8.

You will receive special blessings

1990
A week before I went to Medjugorje.

I was told by Holy Mother, **"You will go to Medjugorje and you and your friend will receive special blessings but in different ways."** All the time I was there I was in great pain in my shoulder (arthritis). The first day we met two American women and it was their last day there. They asked us what had brought us there. So I told them of my wanting to find out if the voices and messages which were coming to me were genuine or not. Then one of the women took my hands and asked me with great faith, if I would ask Our Lady for a message for her. I became very embarrassed and shied away. But she insisted and pleaded with me to pray there and then and said it doesn't matter if nothing happens. So this woman's faith moved me as she believed more than I. So I did pray in my mind and I knelt down in front of Our Lady and prayed for this woman. To my great surprise I heard Our Lady say, **"Tell these two wonderful people My Son has called them here to do His will. This work that they do will be for the salvation of their souls and I will be with them to the end."** When I told them this one of the women shouted with joy and hugged and kissed me. I did not want this and it embarrassed me greatly as I could hardly believe it myself. I saw my friend looking at me in disbelief and this made me feel uncomfortable as I did not want any attention. I knew all the credit for any good should not go to me but to Our Lady, so this always made me feel uncomfortable.

9.

I am Lord and I am here

1990

Dear Diary,

It was on the first trip to Medjugorje at six in the morning, I went into the bathroom. I was just about to have a shower when in my mind I saw my friend rushing in calling my name and asking me to quickly come out onto the balcony. No sooner had I seen it in my mind, when it happened. So I quickly went out to see what she was so excited about. She pointed to the sky and the sun was changing to different colours. It seemed a Host had formed in front of the sun and black dots were coming out from the sun to the sides, then a cross appeared in the sun and at the centre was a beating heart. My reaction was that I fell on my knees crying, hardly believing my eyes. This then disappeared, and there appeared a dark figure, a silhouette of Jesus with His arms outstretched and staff in His right hand. He said to me, **"Go forth and tell everyone I am the Lord and I am here."** Then I saw my whole life's suffering ahead of me all at once. At this I nearly fainted with fright and despair. I was thinking: why me? I will never survive this. Then I heard a voice say, **"Do not distress or worry yourself, I will give you the necessary grace to endure each trial."** I felt greatly comforted and then the whole thing disappeared.

My friend saw things in the sky much the same as I, but did not hear anything. The next day I went to see one of the visionaries and she told me Our Lady would give me a sign to confirm Her messages to me. The next day we climbed the Hill of Apparitions, I wanted to go barefoot as a sacrifice to Jesus for all He suffered for us. Because the arthritis in my feet caused me much pain, the cold stones and jagged rocks hurt so much, I asked Holy Mother to help me to make it to the top, and I heard, **"My child, it pains Me to see you do this, sit down"** (there was a big rock right beside us). As I sat I heard, **"Now put your feet on your bag,"** so I did this. Then the thought came to me to open my bag, and when I did everything in my bag had turned from silver to a gold colour, as I had just bought thirty pairs of rosary beads, all silver, and other items, everything had changed colour. With this my friend also took her shoes off and with the excite-

ment we ran to the top. Then I sat down at the shrine on the top of the hill; as I prayed I felt I was in Heaven, the peace and love was so beautiful.

I asked Our Lady why She did not change my friend's beads and give her signs too, as I wanted her to be happy also. Holy Mother said to me, **"I love all My children the same and give to each one different gifts. I give you these signs so that others may believe what you say."** She also told me that my life would never be the same again and said not to be sad leaving Medjugorje, as She would be with me always. This comforted me greatly.

1991

10.

Seek My Sacred Heart

19 January 1991 *Saturday*

Jesus:

"My dear child, some of God's children are in terrible distress because their anger, fear and pain are blocking all the help we can give them. They must surrender to Me, I will give them strength and courage and peace. Tell them to seek My Sacred Heart and they will be consoled. My dear children, love one another as I have loved you. Comfort each other and I will bless you for this as it is My Blessed Mother's wish and Mine that you share your joys and sufferings in this life. Do not be afraid. I will defend your cause and the wicked will not prevail but will be punished. Strive to do good, My children, and I will reward you."

11.

The Gulf war

January 1991

Jesus:

One night I was lying in bed when suddenly, quite unexpectedly, a light descended upon me. At first I was frightened, but this light was warm and loving and I heard a man's voice say, **"I am preparing you for this event so that you will not be in distress when it happens."** Then I saw in front of me a cloud. Inside this cloud I saw the scene of a war. It was like a movie, like watching a film. I saw men on the ground killing one another; there was a lot of bloodshed. I was very distressed. The war in the air had already started and many thought it would end there and quickly. I felt this experience prepared me for a lengthy war on the ground that would follow; I was told to offer my distress.

12.

I will overcome the world

15 February 1991 *Friday* *Friday after Ash Wednesday*

Jesus:

"My children, listen to Me, the Lord, your God speaks. Let not your sins be numerous because there will soon be a great chastisement. Turn back to Me, My children, quickly as Satan is very strong. This is his kingdom. He now rules over much of the world, but My Kingdom is coming. There really is another life. You are just passing through here. Do not let the world deceive you, it does not have anything to offer that is lasting. Store up in Heaven your treasures and soon you will be with Me in Paradise. Believe, My children, justice will come. Take refuge in Me. Do no harm and you will receive a peace this world cannot give you. Come to Me, My children, and I will give you rest. The people of this world will hate you as they hated Me before you, but

do not fear, My child, I have overcome the world. Satan is very powerful, My children, pray the Rosary often. This is a very powerful weapon. Do not concern yourselves with material things. Live simply and go to church as this is the only time when you are in My Real Presence. Go to Confession at least once a month with the intention of changing afterwards."

13.

Prayer will show you the way

21 February 1991 *Thursday* *Thursday after the First Sunday of Lent*

Holy Mother:

"Today I wish you to pray with all your heart. Jesus has a plan for your life, please be guided by Us. Forgive everyone. Do not hate or hold grudges. Offer everything to the Lord, your God. My child, today I want you to think very carefully, you have a decision to make. I will help you to make it. Pray, Jesus will show you the way. I know it is difficult but only prayer will reveal what you need to know, patience is a virtue. Pray to be guided in the right direction."

14.

Pray for Religious martyred for the faith

22 February 1991 *Friday 7.00 pm* *Feast of the Chair of St. Peter the Apostle*

A Vision

In the middle of the Rosary, I had a vision of a nun in one of these war-torn countries where missionaries go in Europe. This nun was martyred for her faith, and suffered for her faith. The scene I saw was terribly disturbing; I see the nun forced to the ground and a rebel or terrorist take advantage of her. During

this she is praying and offering all to Jesus, as she suffers. Then I knew she is killed, but I do not see it. After this I realize I must pray for the Religious, Priests and nuns who are being persecuted for their faith, or martyred for their faith. I feel very distressed after this and Our Lady says, Jesus wishes to give me a deeper understanding of why more prayer is needed and I am to offer my distress to Jesus as a sacrifice.

15.

Trust in Me

3 March 1991 *Sunday* *Third Sunday of Lent*

Jesus:

"Do not be disheartened, all will be well. Do not let your heart be heavy, My yoke is light. Forgive all offenders and yield not to evil. Pray always to be given strength against the Evil One. I will send you what you need to help you through. Be not afraid, remember I am with you always. Yield to My will and your heart will rejoice. Pray."

16.

Have devotion to My Sacred Heart

4 March 1991 *Monday* *St. Casimir Optional Memorial*

Jesus:

"Dear child, I will help you during your trials, be guided by Me. I am strengthening you for a mission of love, reverence and devotion to My Sacred Heart. Do not fail Me. Believe always and pray to keep the Wicked One from getting his way. I will protect you and your family, but pray always, and praise and thank the Lord who loves you dearly. Fight for goodness, My child, be strong and courageous and I will give you wisdom."

17.

Talk often about My Son to the children

4 March 1991 *Monday* *St. Casimir*
Optional Memorial

Holy Mother:

"Protect your children and help them to grow towards the light. Talk often about My Son and raise them to love and honour Him, as this is pleasing to Me. God bless you, My child, We are with you always. Pray for the world as I need My children all around Me.

Tell .... she is in My heart always and her pain is for My Son's glory. Her endurance is precious and the Most High will console her and give her strength to continue her journey to Me."

Jesus (this is still addressed to .... above):

"She has My Blessed Mother's protection always and do not worry about your sister. I will help her to rebuild her life and she will one day praise and thank Me for it. Go in peace to love and serve the Lord. Blessed be God forever."

18.

Read the Bible each day

10 March 1991 *Sunday* *Fourth Sunday of Lent*

Holy Mother:

"My child, please do not listen to everyone, follow your conscience.* **Continue to pray. Jesus will answer you soon, do not be afraid, We are still with you. Create an active conscience each day (meaning read the Bible), and believe and put it into practice. Decide what you want from life** (understood to mean something that is pleasing to God), **and do not be afraid to attain it. Follow your heart's desire.****

* *Conscience, of course, needs the guidance of the Church.*

** *This was a personal instruction in a particular situation.*

Forgive yourself. Believe in yourself and fear not, My love is sufficient for now."

19.

The greatest love of all is to abandon yourself to My Son's Holy Will

12 April 1991 *Friday*

Holy Mother:

"My child, I am so sorry you have to go through this pain. My heart will console you, believe Me, My child, I will not abandon you. Be confident and have hope in all circumstances. Jesus loves you, He will not abandon you. The greatest love of all is to abandon yourself to My Son's will and He in His mercy will sustain you."

20.

Fear not

17 April 1991 *Wednesday*

Jesus:

"My child, fear not, I am with you. Be joyful of heart in spite of your difficulties. This will help you to cope better, and peace will flow from My heart to yours. Believe more and I will heal you." (And here the hymn "Peace is flowing like a river" comes to my mind.)

21.

Purgatory

23 April 1991 *Tuesday, St. George, Martyr Optional Memorial*

I was in the middle of the Rosary, as I was meditating on the sorrowful mysteries with my eyes closed as I could pray better this way, when I felt the room spin. I opened my eyes and the spinning stopped. At first I suspected morning sickness, as I was in the early stages of my pregnancy. However, I decided to persevere with the Rosary. Then I seemed to be spinning downwards, like in a whirlpool, when suddenly I was in this dark smokey grey place and I saw a sea of people's faces. It was like the living dead. They were all crying, whining and moaning. All were calling to me trying to touch me, as if they were in agony, suffering and pleading with me to help them. It was the most horrible place, I was terrified.

Then I am in a different place, terribly hard to explain, but I feel the sorrow so unbearable. I felt like my heart would burst with grief, I was inside Our Lady's Heart, and She said to me, **"These are all the suffering souls, see the sorrow of My heart and console Me."** I had read many times of the sorrow of Our Lady's Heart, but now I realize it is like the death of one of my children magnified a million times. This is the sorrow She feels as so many of Her children cannot be with Her in Heaven, so I wanted to pray continuously from morning and night, just to console Her and to help release some of them. Now I have a much greater understanding of what a horrible suffering the souls in Purgatory have and that it is within the power of all to help them by prayer. How much Our Lady suffers, I cried for days begging and pleading with Her to forgive me for not realizing how much She suffers and for not praying as much as I should. If only we knew the value of prayer, we could stop wars, lessen chastisements, console Our Blessed Mother and Jesus and save so many souls from Purgatory, and so many people on earth.

22.

Pray for souls in Purgatory

5 May 1991 *Sunday* *Sixth Sunday in Paschal Time*

A dream

In my dream, I am in my bedroom talking with a girlfriend. I am making the bed and when I pull the covers back there is my grandfather lying in the bed and he says, "Surprise"; I nearly fainted with fright. I noticed he was glowing with a beautiful radiance all about him. He was ecstatic and he kept saying, thank you, thank you, I am so happy and he kept hugging me constantly. I was embarrassed because in real life he is a very reserved man not given to open affection, so I knew he was happier than I had ever known him to be. He is dead eleven years I might add. Then he said, "I am going to see your mother" (my grandmother, I called her "mother" because she had partly raised me). He behaved like he had not seen her in a long time.

Again his joy was so touching it makes me want to cry just thinking of it. He had a child's small teddy bear in his arm and he never referred to it, so I felt it acknowledged the baby I was carrying. I said to him, "Mother will be so pleased to see you, she has been missing you so much," again he kept hugging me and repeating how happy he was. When I awoke, I was so moved about how real it seemed. He really seemed to be in my room. When I said to my husband, "Quick, what date is it?" It was 5th May, the eleventh anniversary of his death and I had forgotten. Then I suddenly remembered, that at Mass every day, I had been saying a special prayer to Jesus for the souls in Purgatory. Then it hit me: Oh!! Maybe he was in Purgatory all that time and Jesus is releasing him on his anniversary and he came back to thank me. I cried much that day and I was in some state of shock because it seemed he had been in Purgatory so long, but I was also happy that he had now gone to Heaven. Now I realize how happy souls are when they are released from Purgatory. This makes me want to pray more for them.

23.

Do not be discouraged

1 July 1991 *Monday 9.00 pm* *Monday of the Thirteenth Week of the Year*

Holy Mother:

"My child, I need your prayers, say at least three Rosaries each day to ensure protection from the Evil One. My child, time is short. Please do not worry or be discouraged, I will pray fervently for you and your intentions to My Son. Please heed Me as God is already too much offended."

24.

Offer all to Jesus

1 July 1991 *Monday*

Holy Mother:

"My daughter, do not worry, I will be with you in everything today, guiding you. The Holy Spirit will help you during your teaching, do not be discouraged, Satan is trying to stop you. Consecrate yourself to Me and offer all to Jesus. Go about your duties and leave it in My Son's hands. Thank you."

25.

For the world

1 July 1991 *Monday 10.30 pm*

Holy Mother:

"My children, please do not fight, My Son will be very much offended if you do. Do not give the Wicked One his way. Help Me please, My children, My heart breaks.

Please console Me and do not offend Me any more. I wish for peace, not violence, please pray for guidance and to be led by the Spirit. Place your hope in the things above and your life will change." *

26.

Do not let your heart be troubled with worry

3 July 1991 *Wednesday* *Feast of St. Thomas, Apostle*

I prayed this before I received the following message:

"I stand before You now, Lord, in all Your Majesty. I humbly beg for Your help and comfort. I constantly need Your help. Please console me and give me a stronger faith. Please tell me what to do. I feel confused, please give me wisdom and understanding and help me to praise Your name forever."

Holy Mother:

"My child, do not worry, all will be well. I am with you, your suffering will only be temporary but how much better you will be for it. Please pray to Me more as My heart desires it as does My Son's. At present, My child, patience is all that is required. Show everyone your love and let them see your goodness. I will give you all you need to sustain you in life. Do not let your heart be troubled with worry. I will never abandon you."

* *Geraldine felt that it was important to emphasize that this message is for all God's children.*

27.

Yield to My will and your heart will rejoice

12 August 1991 *Monday of the Nineteenth Week of the Year*

Jesus:

"Do not be disheartened, all will be well. Do not let your heart be heavy, My yoke is light. Forgive all offenders and yield not to evil. Pray always to give you strength against the Evil One. I will send you what you need to help you through. Be not afraid and remember, I am with you always. Yield to My will and your heart will rejoice. PRAY!"

28.

Jesus, a Fountain of Love

24 September 1991 *Tuesday*

It is the first night of a Religious Seminar, a Priest is speaking and I hear this:

Jesus:

"Come, My children and fill My heart with love. I am here among you. Listen to My sons as I guide their every word. Tonight, My children, I wish to express My love in a special way. Blessed are you who come here tonight. Come, come to the fountain and I will fill you with good things."

29.

Pray for peace, love and goodness

8 October 1991 Tuesday

During a Seminar

Holy Mother:

"My dearest child, fear not, I am with you. I see you suffer and I long to console you. Offer all to My Son in whom we are redeemed. Dear child, when they insult you, smile, offer it for the sins in the world. Come to Me and I will give you the grace to overcome. .... has been sent to help and protect you and he is My faithful servant. Pray for him, he suffers much. He is a good person also, and truly My son. I love him and bless him and all he does. He will receive a great reward in Paradise. Stay close to him and take in his spirit. I wish to use you to bring souls to Me in the Seminar. Do not leave it, I chose you for this work. Do not worry or fear, the Holy Spirit will speak through you. Pray for those who persecute you and make peace with all.

Tell My daughter .... I love her, and do not judge each other. Love and encourage each other. Pray for one another and together. My children, you will be put to the test and persecuted, expect it and welcome it and God will bless you and your crown of glory awaits you. I love you. Pray, pray, pray together for one another and for all your needs. Offer your lives as a sacrifice. .... will always give you much joy and was sent to help you in difficult times. Pray for your family that the Holy Spirit will guide and protect them. Pray for evil in the world to cease and for the conversion of sinners. Pray for Priests and all Religious. Pray for the fruits of the Holy Spirit, for peace, love and goodness." (I think of the hymn "Father, I thank you for all you have done".)

30.

Do not despair

12 October 1991 *Saturday* *Twenty Seventh Week of the Year*

In Hospital

I am in hospital, six months pregnant with my sixth child (one died and is in Heaven – a girl); they tell me I am in labour and the baby will not survive. My heart is breaking. I love this child so much I would gladly give my life for it. I am begging and pleading with Jesus for mercy, as I can feel him kicking and full of life, even though my water has broken. Up until this point I had taken the baby for granted. Now I am faced with its death and suddenly nothing else matters, except trying to hang onto this life inside me. I cherish every moment, I talk to it and sing beautiful love songs to it, every moment is precious. All the while I am pleading with Jesus to spare it so we can share all our love. At that moment I contemplate how can anyone ever say life is not precious, it's priceless. While in prayer, I am shown in my spirit or soul a vision of a little fair haired boy about 1½ years old (pudgy) plump running to my husband. This little boy is full of love and affection. I remember feeling my husband's love for him. (Then I knew he would make it. *"Forgive me, Jesus, for doubting You, can You ever forgive me for having so little faith."*)

Holy Mother:

After prayer I hear, **"God is using you, teaching you, He is showing you the way, do not despair. Jesus knows what is best for you. So whatever happens now is in His hands, it is His will. Believe and say: with God's help I can do anything. Love your husband and pray to God for him. Be patient and kind, pray for him constantly so that God will protect him, he loves you very much. Help him by being considerate and supportive. Be a good wife and try to keep the peace with the children, I will help you. The Lord will bless you abundantly when this trial is over, offer it all to us and the greatest joy will be yours. This child in your womb is special** (the name

John comes to mind) so **I will call him Jonathan.*** **Give your children your love and affection, as they need you. Your vocation in life is to bring souls to God. We give you a great joy and a new life** (referring to the baby). **I will protect you and your family. Have no fear, the Evil One will not harm you. I will crush the head of Satan under your feet. Pray continuously, I love you always."**

31.

Do not be worried

2 November 1991 *Saturday* *Commemoration of All Souls*

Holy Mother:

"My child, Jesus will guide you in all things, do not be worried or concerned about anything, trust in My Son, because He wants only what is best for you. Dear child, Satan roams around like a roaring lion waiting to devour you. Protect yourself, wear holy blessed objects. Pray, use holy water more, invoke the protection of My Son's precious blood. Pray to St. Michael for protection. Rejoice in the blessings God has given you, as this is pleasing to Him. Tell all Our sons and daughters of My great love for them. I only wish to save them – the light of God will shine upon them if they repent.

Pray for My son .... as he has great trials ahead of him. Pray for your homeland as Satan is tearing it apart. Tell My children the love of My heart will guide and protect them and also comfort them."

---

* *Later I was told this child would bring great love to me amid suffering. His love will help me very much. (I named him after John the Apostle, who stood with Mary at the foot of the Cross; but I decided to call him Jonathan rather than John, because I liked the name better.)*

1992

32.

Pray more often, you will see a difference in your life

13 February 1992 *Thursday*

Holy Mother:

"My dear child, thank you for your prayers. I need them so much. Please try to pray more often, and you will see a difference in your life. Dear child, be on your guard, Satan is very strong and wants to destroy you. Be guided by Me. Be at peace and pray always to be delivered from evil. My dear child, you have My protection, I will not let any harm come to you. Jesus will console your heart; be joyful in all your troubles and let the world see the peace Jesus sends you. You will have more to suffer, dear child, but please do not get upset. You have My promise, I will give you special graces during this time to sustain you. Do it with a good heart because the reward is great. Come to Me and I will free you from your burdens and gladden your heart. I will help you to rise above every situation and save you from difficulties. Pray more and go to daily Mass and all will go well with you. Be patient, kind and understanding and wait for God to act. He surely will and soon. Fear not, but rejoice in the Lord. He is merciful."

33.

Console your sorrowful Mother

14 February 1992 *Friday* *Memorial of Sts. Cyril and Methodius*

Geraldine: *"Holy Mother, do You have a message?"*

Holy Mother:

"Oh yes, My child, write for souls.

Dear children, your Holy Mother speaks to you. Children so dear to My heart, help Me please, I beg you, quickly, I tell you I suffer so much. Go to everyone you meet and tell them the Lord is coming. Oh My children, My sorrow is immense, I see so much catastrophe ahead of you, come quickly to Me all of you for protection. Pray, pray as never before. Help and console one another. I love you all and want you close to Me to save you from the Evil One who hates you and wants to destroy you and your families. Receive the Sacraments daily, time is of the essence. My Son's wrath is about to come upon the whole world, pray, pray and offer all in reparation, pray more, love more, suffer more. Walk with your Mother the road to Calvary along with My Divine Son, Jesus. My children, God has sent Me to warn you, listen to the voice of the prophets,* as you cannot imagine what the Father has prepared for those who offend Him continuously. Pray, I beg you, for My lost children (here Our Lady is crying and is so pitiful, I feel so sorry for Her as Her heart is breaking). **My beloved children who are faithful to Me, console your sorrowful Mother in constant prayer, penance, reparation and fasting. I bless you in the name of the Father and of the Son and of the Holy Spirit. Amen."**

34.

Pray more

28 February 1992 *Friday 9.00 pm* *After the Seventh Sunday of the Year*

I was reading in my room on my own, when I looked up at a picture I have on my door of Our Lady of Medjugorje. I got a terrible fright as the face was real now and She was crying and very sorrowful. She said, don't read so much and could I pray a lot more as Jesus and Herself are very, very sad because of the state the world is in. She was very gentle and serene and sad and I heard Her voice interiorly, then it stopped.

* *Those who genuinely bear God's message for the world today.*

35.

Repent now

4 April 1992 *Saturday* *After the Fourth Sunday of Lent*

Jesus:

"Dear daughter, My beloved Mother and I are present, be not afraid, I hold you in the palm of My hand. We are so very much offended, My child, by the sins of the world, oh, how My heart grieves (here I feel Jesus' pain and sorrow)**. Many souls are doomed to perdition. How it grieves Me to see this. Console Me, My child, as the pain is unbearable. Why are they so blind, why do they not listen to Me and My Blessed Mother, who loves them with a love beyond their imagination? The greatest joy awaits them in Paradise if only they would repent and turn away from sin. Oh, the sorrow in My poor Mother's Heart! Console Her, My child, as She suffers greatly. Give some consolation to your Blessed Mother. My children, why do you deceive yourselves? Don't you know the Kingdom of God is upon you** (i. e. God's visitation in justice)**? Repent now while there is still time. Weep, My children, for your families, as the earth and Heavens above will shake to their very foundations with a terror the world has never known; woe to the wicked as their fate is terrible. Pray, pray, pray continuously to lessen the punishment as you cannot imagine what God will send. But fear not, My blessed beloved ones, who suffer for My sake, be not afraid, I will be with you in all things. Come close to My Sacred Heart and I will comfort you. Do all in My name and I will bless you for this and the greatest joy shall await you. You will glorify My Father in Heaven by your sacrifices. Do much penance, pray, fast, tell My Priests I love them and I suffer for them greatly. Arm yourselves urgently with My Holy Mother's Rosary, as the Prince of Darkness is unchained from the abyss. In the Rosary you will find protection and consolation. The time is at hand, My loved ones, comfort one another, pray with and for each other. Suffer for souls, My chosen one, and the greatest joy in Heaven will be yours for all eternity."**

36.

Take up your cross and carry it with joy

5 April 1992 *Sunday* *Fifth Sunday of Lent*

Holy Mother:

"My child, how My maternal heart feels for you. You must suffer this for My Son, give all to Him who suffered so much for you. Forgive all who hurt and offend you and Jesus will forgive them too and bless you for it. My dearest, dearest child, take comfort in Me, I will sustain you in all your difficulties.

Tell .... that I am close to her and love her and not to be afraid, Satan will flee if she opens her heart more. This prayer group will bring great joy and glory to My Son, Jesus. Offer all in prayer, My children, suffer gladly, My children, for the sins in the world, give My Son your pain and a crown of glory will await you.

My child, do not let Satan blind you, he will try to deceive you, pray over misunderstandings and doubts, and My Son will enlighten you. My child, do you wish to suffer for Jesus? If so, then take up your cross and carry it with joy." But Our Lady also asked if I would accept all Jesus wishes to give me, and I asked, if He would also give me all I need to endure. As I speak there is a severe pain in my left hand and foot. When I prayed for guidance, Our Lady told me it was from God, as He needs souls to ease or share His pain and this in turn comforts Him and helps save souls. Tonight during the Rosary, I burst into tears and feel a terrible pain in my heart, as the closer I come to my Mother in Heaven the harder I find it to bear being away from Her. I miss Her so much, even now my heart aches and longs to be with Them. Then Holy Mother assures me She and Jesus are here with me and to rejoice, as many people cannot hear Her, and Jesus gave me this grace because He knew how much I would long to be with Them after seeing Them and feeling Their Love; and I was to praise and thank Him as this was pleasing to Him. The baby is crying now so I have to finish.

37.

Seek the Kingdom of God

9 April 1992 *Thursday, After the Fifth Sunday of Lent*

Jesus:

"By their fruits you will know them. Be not misled by anyone. My child, encourage one another, lift each other up in prayer. Do not desire to glorify yourselves, but only My Father through Me. Seek the Kingdom of God, My children, and the rest will be given unto you."

38.

When friends fail

9 April 1992 *Thursday, After the Fifth Sunday of Lent*

Holy Mother:

"Dear child, I am with you, do not be discouraged, I have spoken to Jesus, My Son, He will help you. If friends fail you, do not worry, Jesus will light the Way." (Now I feel so peaceful and relieved and full of joy. Thank you, Jesus, thank you. Here I am praising and thanking Jesus for His goodness, and for the beautiful message from Holy Mother, and I thank Him for Holy Mother.)

39.

Do not dwell on negative things

9 April 1992 *Thursday, After the Fifth Sunday of Lent*

Holy Mother:

"Forgive Me, My child, for today I am so sad. My Immaculate Motherly Heart is so grieved by the state

of the world, I am full of sorrow, My heart bleeds for My children. Pray for peace and one another. My children, unite yourselves to Jesus. My child, in all you do, comfort each other in trials and praise the Lord, your God, as this is very pleasing to Him. Lift up all your joys and sorrows to the Lord and He will sustain you. Thank you, My faithful children in whom My heart finds much joy, thank you.**

My children, I wish all of you to be united to Me and My Divine Son in prayer, offer all and My Son will bless you for this. Suffer all for souls, My children, and do not be afraid. I am very close to you, do not dwell on negative things, as this is how the faithless live. Lift up your hearts, minds and souls to the Lord and He will bless you for this. Be cheerful always and rejoice in God from whom all good things come. Read the Living Word each day and put it into practice. Do not be fearful, as this will prevent My love from reaching you. Trust all to Me and the Lord, your God. Bless everyone you meet and all will go well with you. Teach your children all about My Son and they will grow to love Him."

40.

Abortion

12 April 1992 *Sunday* *Palm Sunday*

Today I am terribly distressed. I am crying because I had a very disturbing dream this morning. In this dream my husband and I are looking out of a window to what appears to be an alleyway or a backstreet laneway, with a lot of bins for rubbish all in one area. There seemed to be broken dolls with no clothes, some in bins, others on the ground. From a distance it looks like a dolls' hospital. Some have no arms, some no legs, all are broken. Then I decide to go down closer. As I have a closer look, to my horror, I see the face of one of the so-called dolls that it is the face of a little human baby, its face beautifully formed and it is dead. I look all around me and there are hundreds of dead mutilated babies lying in bins and on the ground. Realizing this I become hysterical, screaming and horrified at this sight. I cry

out to my husband, "Someone has murdered all these babies." Crying and heartbroken I look at the poor mutilated bodies (of these beautiful babies) lying in front of me. Suddenly a window appears in front of me and as if my grief were not enough, I see two women in this room cutting up a baby on a table. Again I cannot find words to describe my horror and the pain in my heart as I screamed to my husband, "They are killing these babies." I screamed so much I felt the whole world must have heard. Then I heard a voice say, **"These are all the aborted babies, pray for them."** Also, I realized the two women were experimenting on human life, so I knew I had to pray also for test tube experiments, etc. (i. e. to pray for the prevention of abortions and those experimentations on human life, which are against God's law, and for all the people involved). Then just as I think it is over, I leave the scene only to return and find this laneway cleaned up and there is no longer anyone in the room where they had been experimenting. Then I realized that fearing that they might be exposed, these things are done mostly in secret behind closed doors and afterwards all evidence is removed and everything is cleaned away. I wake up realizing, in all my prayers for everyone, I had forgotten about the unborn babies murdered in the womb and now Jesus had reminded me to pray for them.

41.

Pray more to overcome evil

15 April 1992 *Wednesday* *Wednesday of Holy Week*

At night as I try to pray I am tormented by demons, in that, whenever I try to close my eyes, horrible ugly evil creatures appear before my eyes and insult me, laugh at me, jeer and mock me. But it only makes me pray more to overcome. On some other nights, while half asleep, I feel as though I am in two worlds. I am aware of many people in this other world singing and praising God very beautifully and I am drifting in and out of this other world, which I believe is Heaven.

42.

I am here

17 April 1992 Good Friday

Today is my birthday and it also turned out to be a very holy day. To start the day the whole family watched "The Miracle of Fatima". After this we all did the Family Rosary, then we watched "The Greatest Story ever Told". Some of the family then went for a drive in the car.

Now it is 2.45 pm, close to Our Lord's crucifixion, so I say, "We will say another rosary." I lit the candles and we knelt down. I had brought out my statues of the Sacred Heart and of the Crucified Christ, and I put them next to the statue of Mary. When we had said the Rosary and Novena to the Sacred Heart, it was 3.00 pm. As I am kneeling down I feel a very strong urge to prostrate myself on the floor in front of the statues. As I am praying, I suddenly start praying in a different language. It was not the normal speaking in tongues, it was very powerful or like a fluent Hebrew. I felt as though another powerful person was inside me worshipping Jesus with tremendous adoration.* I felt as though I was only the instrument. Then to my amazement, I see a vision in front of the statue, like a scene from a movie, only it is Calvary. I see Jesus on the cross and a few people at the foot of the cross, but I can only see the back of them. It is cloudy and darkish, the sky is reddish like evening, and Jesus dies in front of me. Then it vanishes and I see Jesus' face in front of me and it comes closer to me and His eyes seem to say, I'm alive, I'm here. This only lasted a moment. I felt a mixture of shock and excitement and peace.

---

* *Maybe this is an experience of the Holy Spirit, cf. Romans 8:26: "The Spirit too comes to help us in our weakness. For when we cannot choose words properly, the Spirit Himself expresses our plea in a way that could never be put into words."*

43.

Arm yourselves with My Holy Rosary

24 April 1992 *Friday 12.30 pm* *Friday after Easter*

Holy Mother:

"My child, I, your Blessed Mother am present, do not be afraid. Satan cannot harm you as you have My motherly protection. But you must still arm yourself with prayer, especially My Holy Rosary. My daughter, please be guided by Me, do not be deceived by the world. My daughter, prostrate* yourself before Me and console Me as My heart aches for My children. My Holy Angels are present in veneration. I wish to make known through you the sufferings of my Immaculate Heart. Tell My beautiful children how much I love them and long to teach them. Oh, My child, the pain in My heart is unbearable, help Me, I suffer greatly. Pray, pray, pray** (here my heart is breaking as I feel Our Lady's sorrow). **Oh, My daughter, why do they not listen to My words. I want only to save them from eternal perdition. The Holy Father will have much to suffer. I wish you, My daughter, to fast three times a week to console Me in My pain, do not worry, I will help you. Thank you, My child, for listening. Go in peace! Amen."**

---

* *"Prostrate" – This bodily posture requested by Our Lady expresses humility, gratitude for the graces given by God, deep sympathy at Our Lady's sorrows and to show that we wish to console Her and to make reparation. This is the way Geraldine understood this.*

** *Some Holy Angels seem to be present wherever Our Blessed Lady goes and they are present in the sense of veneration and attending on the Blessed Virgin.*

44.

Be a good example

28 April 1992 *Tuesday* *St. Peter Chanel Optional Memorial*

Holy Mother:

This morning after Mass, I asked our Holy Mother to bless me today, as I am starting the Holy Rosary in the church tonight and I was not going to bring all my family for fear the young ones would distract me, so our Blessed Mother said, **"Do not worry, I will be standing beside you guiding your every word, and the Holy Angels* will be present. The Evil One wants to stop you. But you have My protection. I want you to bring your family with you as I wish you to set an example to all the families in the parish and to be a light for them. I will guide everything."**

45.

Put on the armour of God

29 April 1992 *Wednesday* *St. Catherine of Siena Memorial*

I was having a very strange time for at least one week. At 3 o'clock every night I would be woken up by voices in another world constantly telling me to put on the armour of God**, as I was about to commence battle. At this time, Mary appeared in a dream standing at the bottom of a stairway with St. Michael at one side and the Angel Gabriel at the other side and She was crying, asking me to help Her and to pray to these Angels and the Saints. There were hundreds of people along the stairway and behind Her. I felt I was being awoken during the night to pray.

---

* *Holy Angels: referring to some Angels, e. g. the Angels who usually accompany Our Lady, Geraldine's Guardian Angel and the Guardian Angels of the other people present.*

** *Ephesians 6:10-17*

46.

A dream

30 April 1992 *Thursday St. Pius V, Pope*
Optional Memorial

God the Father:

In my dream, I see God the Father Almighty, and He calls a woman named .... He says .... come forth, and His voice is like thunder and His presence so terrifying. I am thinking at this moment (God help us on the day of His judgement), as I see His Almighty power as He seemed to be looking over the whole universe, we were smaller than insects in His Almighty presence. (God:) **"..........., come forth,"** He says. Here I feel His Fatherly love for this person and He commands her to go forth and give His love to all (i. e. to persevere in faith and love and to spread the love of God to others).

47.

Pray for My Priest sons

April/May 1992

Jesus:

Another day I cried as I see a Priest rush so fast through Mass, we could not understand him.

I felt hurt for Jesus, but Jesus said, **"This is My beloved son whom I love, do not say anything, just pray for him."** I felt Jesus' love for him. If this Priest only knew how he is loved, he would have so much more reverence.

48.

Be kind to everyone

April/May 1992

Holy Mother:

Another time, Our Lady reminded me to be extra kind to my husband, bring him a small gift and show him more attention. She also says to pray for my workmates and bless everyone and give or love them with Her love. One night after months of getting up a few times in the night for the baby, this night I resented it and I heard very firmly, **"This is a child of God, treat him as such."**

49.

Appease My anger

April/May 1992

God the Father:

Another time, I was finding it extremely hard to get to Holy Mass in the mornings, and I prayed and struggled, and one morning I heard very clearly God the Father's voice say, **"Find the necessary strength to appease My anger..."** in voice so serious, I jumped out of bed to go – His voice was so commanding and full of authority, I didn't dare to question.

50.

Pray fifteen Mysteries daily

30 April 1992 *Thursday* *St. Pius V, Pope Optional Memorial*

Holy Mother:

After Communion

"My daughter, was I not present and guiding your every word at the Rosary? Thank you, My daugh-

ter. And now I wish to ask you to say the fifteen Mysteries or Decades of the Rosary each day in reparation for sins, to console My Immaculate Heart. Thank you, My child." (In my spirit, I see Her bless Jonathan and myself.)

51.

Seek to do the will of My Son

1 May 1992 *First Friday 9.45 am* *St. Joseph the Worker Optional Memorial*

Holy Mother:

"My Son wishes to use you in a special way. It does not matter where you go as long as you bring souls back to Jesus. This work will be to your eternal salvation, and to My Son's great glory and honour. Go forth in My name and may God of all goodness be with you in everything. Do not worry what the world thinks of you. You will be persecuted for your faith as My Son was before you, but seek only to do the will of My Divine Son."

52.

I am with you in suffering

6 May 1992 *Wednesday* *Third Week of Easter*

Holy Mother:

"My child, do not weep in sorrow. My Son wishes to use your suffering to appease His anger. Offer it all to Me, dear daughter, for the sins in the world committed against the Sacred Heart of Jesus. I will give you the graces necessary to endure each trial, do not weep. You have great favour with your heavenly Father. Do not worry, be glad, My child. When you suffer for God's sake, Heaven rejoices.

Weep not for yourself, but for Me. I am very happy this day as many prayers were said, favours granted and hearts touched and opened. Thank you, daughter, for making this possible. You wonder why. You seem worried and concerned for the future – don't be, leave all in My Son's sure hands and tell Him all your needs. Don't cry, My child, I am with you and you are in My heart. You are not alone.

My child, I love you with a great love, please feel My Motherly and everlasting love for you (here I cry as I feel Her love)**. I am with you in your suffering. It is not in vain. My child, I wish to place My arms around you and caress you till your pain subsides. I love you immensely. My heart is breaking, watching you suffer, as it did when My Son died. I pray to the heavenly Father and My Son to sustain you in all your difficulties. I am constantly at your side, and in all things I am preparing you. I suffer so much I need you to help Me. Please snatch souls from the fires of Hell while there is still time. Store your treasures in Heaven, do not worry, I will help and provide for you. Place your trust in Me and pray more for your husband and children."**

53.

Consecrate yourselves to Me

8 May 1992 *Friday 9.30 pm*

Holy Mother:

"My child, bless yourself five times in remembrance of My Son's Holy Wounds. Dear daughter, write down what you hear. Today I wish to convey to you My heart's desires, firstly, as you know this is the first Friday of the month. I wish all My children to make reparation for sins in the world in a most special way. I wish all to consecrate their hearts to Me and My Divine Son Jesus. Do not hesitate, My children, to come closer to Me as I am full of grace. Pray always to be delivered from evil. Thank you, My child."

54.

Be My witness to the world that I do exist

24 May 1992 *Sixth Sunday of Easter*

Jesus:

"My child, unite yourself to Me and fulfil My Holy Will and I will raise you up on the last day. My child, your mission in life is to bring souls to Me. This grace I gave you was not for you alone, but for the good of everyone so that you will be My witness to the world that I do exist. I have called you by your name, daughter."

55.

I am close to you

24 May 1992 *Sixth Sunday of Easter*

Holy Mother:

"It is I, Holy Mother, do you feel at peace, you already have received a grace today? Can you feel your broken heart mended once again? I just want you to know, I am close and I love you. Pray for ...."

Geraldine: *"Holy Mother, do I go public?"*

Holy Mother:

"First see your Spiritual Director, he will guide you. Jesus will work through him, be at peace. My child, stay and be united in peace and love."

(At the advice of my Spiritual Director, I shared some of the messages with people in the prayer group I attended.)

56.

Turn off your television

11 June 1992 *Thursday* *St. Barnabas, Apostle Memorial*

Jesus:

"Oh My daughter, be silent and know that I am God. Have I ever abandoned you? Am I not at this present moment standing by you? Be not afraid for I am within you. Have courage, My child, and abide in Me who am all love. I have not forsaken you. The torment your soul has suffered is also a purification, offer all to My Heavenly Father for all needy humanity. Beloved daughter, I see you suffer greatly, but do not distress yourself, I will be your shining light. You still doubt. But I understand this and you will grow. Your Spiritual Director will guide and help you greatly. What you will suffer now will not last long. I will triumph in the end, pray much and offer all and this trial will pass quickly. I wish to use you to spread My messages, do not worry, I will show you the way. Just write all I say for now. I will sustain you in everything as you are Mine, you belong to Me and I love you. I will not let you suffer beyond your capacity. I must now let My Holy Mother speak as I feel that you need Her more now."

Holy Mother:

"My child, don't be afraid, Satan cannot harm you. Angels surround you always and especially now. Turn off your television.* Do not be afraid, I have come to comfort you." (Here I am interiorly aware of Our Lady's presence sitting with me on the lounge.) She says, **"Fear not, little one, and be at peace. My Son loves you."**

---

* *Here I feel Our Lady is wanting me to pray more.*

57.

Be at peace and leave everything in My hands

12 June 1992 *Friday 8.30 pm* *Friday after Pentecost*

For ....

Holy Mother:

"My child, thank you for your prayers, questions and curiosity. Dear child, you must pray to My Son, give Him your problems and worries and let His will be done, not yours (allusion to Matthew 26:39)**. Then believe He has answered your prayer and thank Him and let peace and joy come from this. Do not worry, as Jesus and I cannot reach you with fear and worry blocking you. You can say the Novena to the Sacred Heart and ask for the intercession of a Saint on your behalf. Do not be sad, My child, as Jesus will light the way. Leave all in His hands and He will surely bless you. I love you, My child. Go in peace."**

58.

Pray more for the conversion of sinners

3 July 1992 *First Friday* *Feast of St. Thomas, Apostle*

Holy Mother:

"Do not worry, all will go well, I will be present. Fear not, the Holy Spirit will again take control and help you.

It is My wish that you pray more for the conversion of sinners. Pray for discernment."

59.

I know your heart

25 July 1992 *Saturday* *Feast of St. James, Apostle*

Jesus:

"............, My daughter, it is I, Jesus. My child, I love you, be at peace. I know your heart, I have forgiven you your sins. I wish you now to pray for the conversion of .... Pray to My heart, My Mother's heart and the Angels and Saints to ask on your behalf. Lead a good life in so far as you can, to be at peace with Me. Trust in Me to sustain you in everything. I love you and I bless you, go in peace."

60.

Have your homes blessed and have an Enthronement to My Son

25 July 1992 *Saturday* *Feast of St. James, Apostle*

Holy Mother:

"............, My beloved daughter, I see your anxiety, be at peace. I bless your marriage. My daughter, I will arrange everything for you. Have your home blessed, and have an enthronement to My Son done in each of your homes. I desire this, the Evil One will not be so active then. Your decision has greatly pleased Me. I love you, I bless you and I will help you. Go in peace." *

* *This is very important to protect families as Satan is very active in many homes. It was understood that to consecrate families to the Sacred Heart of Jesus and the Immaculate Heart of Mary was also very important.*

61.

Your God is offended

26 July 1992 *Sunday* *Seventeenth Sunday of the Year*

Jesus:

"Daughter, let it be known, your God is being offended daily and I wish My chosen ones to make up for all I am suffering. Tell them to continue to appease My anger, tell the Priests to pray more.

That is all for now, I do not wish to speak anymore on this subject. I love you, My child, suffer with Me for souls."

62.

Satan is blinding even My chosen ones

2 August 1992 *Sunday* *Eighteenth Sunday of the Year*

Holy Mother:

"My daughter, oh how My heart grieves for My children. Satan is blinding even My chosen ones. Be always on your guard, dear children. It pleases My Son, Jesus and Myself that you have started to pray more in groups, especially My Holy Rosary. Thank you, My beloved daughters. Do not be sad or disheartened, I am with you always. Seek refuge in My Immaculate Heart. Love one another as love endures everything. My children, be a light for all who come to you in darkness. Consecrate your hearts to Me and I will protect you from the snares of the Wicked One. Fear not, My Immaculate Heart will triumph. Offer up all your trials as a sacrifice for the sins of the world and Jesus will bless you for this. Thank you."

63.

Our Father in Heaven

6 August 1992 *Thursday* *Feast of the Transfiguration of the Lord*

A dream

In my dream, I am in what seems to be a palace with beautiful rooms of gold, etc. Angels are guiding me through double doors, as each set of doors open, baby Angels open them, I am going through room after room, until I at last reach a room where a man is sitting on a throne. He is like a king and there are lots of people sitting at His feet. I am brought to Him, where there is a place at His feet for me too, and I feel privileged as He is so adored and worshipped. I feel as though He loves me and I am home. He is like a father that welcomes me.

64.

Offer your life for the salvation of souls

12 August 1992 *Wednesday*

Holy Mother:

"I wish .... to seek refuge in My Immaculate Heart. There she will be consoled. My child, never before as now has My heart been so sorrowful. Through your suffering we are united. Please offer this to Me* in reparation for sins in the world and the Lord, your God, will bless you for this. Dear daughter, the time is coming when all mankind will suffer much. But the joy that awaits you is for all eternity. Let this offering of your life to Me be for the salvation of souls. Pray always, receive the Sacraments, so as to receive the graces needed from My Son."

* *Mary is our Heavenly Mother and so She always intercedes for Her children before God. When we offer some good work or suffering and give it to Her, it strengthens Her hand in interceding for us. She brings our good works and offerings to God.*

65.

In pain and suffering I am closest to you

25 August 1992 *Tuesday* *St. Louis*
or St. Joseph Calasanz
Optional Memorial

Holy Mother:

"My daughter, do not worry, I understand your reasons for asking for this message. Tell ...., My Son Jesus and I are very pleased with him, and his purity and innocence. Tell My son I love him greatly and I am close to him in all his suffering and Jesus will reward him greatly for this. I wish his life to be devoted to Us as many of My sons have deserted Me and left the Priesthood. It would make Me very happy if .... would devote his life to Me, although I have given him free will to choose. Be strong, My son, I am close to you always. Pray often and receive the Holy Sacraments frequently and remember My Son in pain and suffering and difficult times. This is when Jesus and I are closest to you. Be good, My son, and honour your parents. Love everyone, and offer all to Jesus. Thank you, My daughter."

66.

Love everyone as I love you

3 November 1992 *Tuesday* *St. Martin de Porres*
Optional Memorial

Jesus:

"My child, do not be discouraged, I will show you the way. Prepare for My Coming, the Kingdom of God is at hand. Persevere in all your trials, I will not test you beyond your capability. It would make Me happy for you to receive the Sacraments daily. In this you will be strengthened and comforted. Your husband is a good man, believe in him and his authority. Support him, encourage him, build up his spirit. Pray for him. I will help you both to come to Me

together, be not afraid or worried about your health or anything. I will provide.

I have given you this baby boy. He will bring much joy to your family, I have blessed his heart. Forgive all wrongs and offer up all to Me. Do this and the greatest joy will be yours. Bear all sufferings with joy. Your vocation* in life is to love, sacrifice and bring souls to Me. I will help you in this, you will glorify Me and My Father in Heaven. My Holy Mother will be close to you in all things. Console Her often as She suffers much. Do penance, pray continuously and I will bless you for this. I love you more than you could imagine. It is one of My greatest desires that you be with Me in Heaven, where all your family wait patiently for you. Oh, My daughter, I fill your heart with My love, give this love to all you meet. Love everyone as I love you, as this is very pleasing to Me."

67.

I want you to offer your life for souls in suffering and prayer

3 November 1992 *Tuesday* *St. Martin de Porres Optional Memorial*

Holy Mother:

"My child, it is I, so do not fear, today I am hurt beyond comprehension. My thoughts are with My Son who suffers most. Pray and offer sacrifices in reparation for the atrocities committed against Him daily. Offer all in reparation and seek to console Him daily as He is greatly offended. I do not wish you to watch television any more, My child, the time has come for continuous prayer as otherwise you will not withstand these evil dark days ahead of you. I want you to offer your life for souls in suffering and prayer. Do not be afraid of anyone. I will give you more graces to endure the snares of the Evil One, who tries to discourage you. This is

* *Your vocation: I. e. within the married state you do love, you do sacrifice and you do bring souls to God.*

why, when you come to Me, you feel peaceful and joyful in spite of your troubles. I wish you to tell My Priest sons how I love them and suffer for them. First, pray to the Holy Spirit to guide you, He will give you the opportunity to proclaim the truth. Now is the time for which I have prepared you to defend My Son and proclaim His name. Now I am calling you to witness for Him as He witnessed for you. I do not ask this in order to condemn but out of love for My children, who are in so much need of the truth. My child, it is true you are called to suffer, but I assure you with My love to sustain you, it will be done joyfully.

Praise your Father always for His wonderful gifts to you. You have been called to lead a pure and holy life, free from the corruption of this world. Go in peace, My child."

68.

My heart bleeds for My chosen children

3 November 1992 *Tuesday* *St. Martin de Porres Optional Memorial*

Holy Mother speaks:

"Oh, My daughter, how you will suffer for souls. Do not be discouraged, I am close to you. Be not afraid, My mantle will protect you. Pray always to be delivered from every evil. My daughter, My heart bleeds* for My chosen children, because you are like lambs among wolves. But the mercy of My Son will sustain you. Tell .... My Immaculate Heart will be her refuge and Jesus, My Son, will pour out His graces on her during her consecration to Me. Do not become disheartened, My children, the consolation that I receive from you will be to your greatest joy in Heaven. Persevere, My children and look towards Heaven during your trials and Jesus will light the way. Offer all to Me for souls and the greatest joy will be yours. Oh My daughter, how My heart**

* *Because Her children will suffer; the innocent will suffer at the hands of wicked people.*

** *When we try to console Our Lady, it means very much to Her; it means much, much more, than we can imagine.*

longs for you to be with Me in Paradise. My love for you is everlasting. Console Me, dear children. Stay close to Me and My Motherly Heart will console you. My love for you is so great you could never comprehend it. Give My love to everyone you meet. Bless everyone and pray more for My lost children."

69.

I wish to embrace you at every moment

3 November 1992 *Tuesday* *St. Martin de Porres Optional Memorial*

Holy Mother:

"My dearest child, it pleases Me so much that you prayed the Holy Rosary in thanksgiving for My Son's goodness toward you. You felt the presence of My Son and it fills My heart with joy that you give Him the adoration and respect which is due to Him. Do not be sad when people receive Him abruptly, just pray for them.

I am tireless*, My child, and I love you and wish to embrace you at every moment. While the faithful are in adoration, My Son will bestow an abundance of graces on those present. Coming here is no accident. I am calling My faithful children here to help Me fulfil My plan for the world. Each will have his own mission with the grace of the Lord to fulfil it. Go forward, My children, with love, patience, fortitude, and perseverance. I will be guiding everything. Trust in My Son and Me. Pray more and offer all."**

* *"Tireless," Our Lady is continually interceding before God on our behalf.*

** *In anticipation of going to Medjugorje, an international place of pilgrimage. This message was given before going.*

70.

Receive the Sacraments daily

12 November 1992 *Thursday* *St. Josaphat Memorial*

Holy Mother:

"My beloved child, you will be a lot more aware of My presence before long. The Lord has plans for your life. Do not worry, He will take care of everything, My child. Can you ever imagine My love for you? But you are in great danger. Satan has terrible diabolical traps in store for you. You must heed My warnings and stay very close to Me always no matter what the situation. I wish you again to receive My Son each day now to build your faith and become stronger, as so many will seek your counsel. You must be guided by Me." (Always in submission to the Church's teaching.)

I asked Holy Mother, *"Have You any messages?"*

Holy Mother:

"My daughter, the main person in My mind right now is you, because I feel at this time you are most in need. My child, you will hear of another death soon. Do not be alarmed, I will take this person into My bosom. You must love one another, as I have loved you all. Again give this love to everyone. Thank you, My child, your prayer consoles Me greatly." *

* *I just had bad news of the death of my Aunt. Shortly afterwards Our Lady warned me to prepare for another death: Then I hear my uncle had drowned, and I was prepared.*

71.

I will never abandon you

23 November 1992 Monday 8.30 pm, St. Clement I, Pope, or St. Columban Optional Memorial

In front of the Blessed Sacrament:

I poured my heart out to Jesus and Mary for help and guidance and I was asking Jesus for a sign to assure me of His presence. In my spirit I saw Our Lady standing beside me, She said not to be discouraged that Jesus would help me, that my tears are Hers and Hers mine and She will never abandon me. She also said, **"You don't listen to Me as much as you used to any more,"** and She asked me to turn off the television and have more quiet time with Jesus and Her in prayer. She comforted me and reassured me everything would be all right and I was never alone. Then She took my two hands in Hers and anointed them with the sign of the cross with oil* and told me, **"With these hands you will do the work of My Son and bring Him to many people"** and She blessed this ministry. Also when She blessed my hands I felt a great heat all through my hands. The next day my prayers were answered in a big way.** She hugged me, and comforted me greatly. I was filled with joy after this.

72.

Satan laughs

November 1992

A dream

In this dream I see the moon with a skeleton's face looking down on the earth. The face has real eyes and was watching everything. When suddenly there was an explosion in the moon

* *She seemed to have some sort of liquid on Her hands (presumed to be oil).*

** *At the time of the message I was very distressed. The next day problems were wonderfully solved.*

and a very evil man appeared, wicked looking. He was laughing loudly, as he watched all the people around me being wicked and hateful, mean, cruel, indifferent and cheating, and this man was laughing as he watched and gloated over the evil in the world. I feel it's Satan gloating over what he feels is his triumph.

73.

The real presence of Jesus in the Eucharist

27 November 1992 *Friday* *Thirty Fourth Week of the Year*

At Jamberoo (On Retreat)

At Holy Mass I am crying because I am asking Jesus to give me back the love I had or felt in His Presence before, and I am looking at all the nuns gathered around the altar. I wish I was them because they are brides of Christ and I wished I was too. Then after the Host, I received the Precious Blood of Jesus and I said, *"I love You."* At that moment Jesus' face appears in front of me. I see Him right in front of me from the shoulders up. I see Him with my spiritual eyes, the eyes of my soul. But I see Him as clearly as I see with my real eyes open.* And I say, *"Jesus, Jesus, You are here, You are really in me,"* and I am crying. The tears are streaming down my face and I am filled with love and joy. But I try to compose myself so I do not draw attention to myself.

November 1992

Several times, at Jamberoo (on retreat), I would open the door to enter my room, when I would hear many evil voices call me disgusting names and telling me to get out, trying to frighten me. As soon as I pray or call on Mary or Jesus they (the evil ones, trying to destroy my peace) realize it is useless.

Dear Diary,

So many supernatural things are happening, I hardly know where to start, reflecting on my retreat at Jamberoo (a Religious Retreat House where there are cottages for retreatants).

---

* *Seeing Jesus like this confirmed my belief in His Real Presence and gave it a whole new meaning.*

74.

Lead good lives

28 November 1992 Saturday

Holy Mother:

After Communion, Our Lady said to me, **"Many people say that Jesus, My Son, has forsaken them.* People pray to Him and wonder why the prayers are not answered. Tell them to ask forgiveness for their sins first, then also, they must lead good lives. When they do this, then Jesus will answer their prayers."**

75.

People must feel the love of My Son in Prayer Groups

30 November 1992 Monday Feast of St. Andrew, Apostle

Today I am filled with a most wonderful peace and joy. It's almost Heavenly. I feel it is a grace or blessing from Jamberoo, or perhaps a prayer answered (as I asked for this feeling back when last I was in the presence of the Lord and today I feel it). Thank You, Jesus. May Your name be praised, adored, worshipped and glorified throughout the world. Then, as I was doing a spiritual exercise, listening to a tape from St. Gertrude, I became aware of the Holy Mother's presence. She spoke to me of many things regarding our prayer group.

Holy Mother:

"I wish this to be a place where people experience the love of My Son. Love one another as I have loved you. Jesus wishes to use you. (Here I feel afraid; because I feel there is suffering involved.) **Do not be concerned as to how, what, where or why. I need only your will. Do you wish to accept all My Son asks of you?** (I reply, *"Holy Mother, I completely trust in You and Your Divine Son. I give you my life, my heart and my soul. Let Your most holy will be done."*) She hugged me and I Her and

* *In the sense that their prayers are not answered.*

I kissed Her. She then showed me a sword in Her heart and said, **"Do you see this heart of sorrow which is so offended by My children? Well, it is My other children such as you who console Me and give Me great joy. Oh, if only all could love Me like this."**

Another time She referred to Herself as: **"I am the Immaculate Conception. There has been no other before or since Me. I wish your life to be pure, My child."** I said, *"Holy Mother, I am married and my husband expects to be loved."* She smiled and said: **"It is possible to be pure inside the Sacrament of marriage. I will teach you to be as pure and as holy as the Saints you honour."** Now, I see with the eyes of my soul, the back of Our Lady ascending a stairway. She has a crown on Her head, and a huge, long and wide cloak hanging from Her shoulders, just like a queen. There are thousands of people along the stairway and at the top, Angels also. It is another world. Then I see Jesus standing at the top of the stairs with His hands outstretched as if embracing the world. There are thousands of people worshipping Him kneeling down and there are clouds in the sky behind Him. He has a long white robe on, gathered with a cord around the waist. His hair is to His shoulders, brown.

Then I feel myself being plunged downwards. I am frightened and I ask Jesus and Mary to be with me, as I am going down and down with great speed. Suddenly my heart leaps with fright as I am plunged into a black hole. I am constantly praying to Jesus and Mary to protect me. I am in a dark place like a cave below the ground, when a huge serpent (with a face like a man) comes around a corner, sneering at me. (The floor of this cave – it was smelly, filthy and disgusting. Then Satan spits in front of me.) He says: "So they send you here to see what it is like." He was hideous, clearly evil. A wicked presence is all around me and on the walls there are faces of people whose heads resemble wild animals. They are shouting at and cursing me. This serpent clearly wanted to harm me. Due to my praying he could not touch me, only call me disgusting names and try to scare me. I hear a noise, and terrified I opened my eyes. I feel sick, terrified, shocked and wanting desperately to share my experience with someone.

30 November 1992 Monday Feast of St. Andrew, Apostle

Dear Diary,

I am so upset, I am in a dreadful state of shock. I feel I am going to die if I don't share my experiences with someone. *"Oh, Jesus, please be my loving guide in all I say, and do not forsake me in my afflictions. Oh, Jesus, please give me strength from You to cope with all this* (the experience of Hell which left me full of fear and anxiety), *and also help me to praise and thank You for all of this. Be my light and guide forever and always. I love You so much."* (I am crying.)

I tried to contact my Spiritual Director but could not reach him. I am so upset. I then hear Our Lady say (after I asked her to help me understand what had happened): **"Because of your sensitivity, we have not shown you everything all at once. My Son has shown you where wicked people go and where the good go. Satan promises his people everything, but then he deceives them. This is where the wicked end up. Offer up this terrible distress to My Son as a sacrifice."** (Here I feel peaceful again and all the agitation leaves me. I feel much better.)

1993

76.

I see My Adversary ready to devour you

2 January 1993 Saturday Sts. Basil the Great and Gregory Nazianzen

Holy Mother:

"Today I wish to tell all My children that as I stand at the dawn of a new year, I await with the greatest sorrow what is ahead of you all. You do not understand or heed My messages of the past. You cannot imagine My distress as I see My Adversary ready to devour you. This is why I ask for more prayers, especially the frequenting of the Sacraments, because the time is very short now and I wish you to be ready and prepared for this day. Please heed My

warning. Pray more so that you will go through the darkness which will come upon you so suddenly. Arm yourselves with My Holy Rosary often, and do not take pride in yourselves, remain humble in all things."

77.

My heart yearns for My beloved little children to console Me more

10 January 1993 *Sunday* *The Baptism of the Lord Feast*

Holy Mother:

"My dear child, I wish to convey to you My innermost feelings. Write this down. I want to tell all My children, do not be afraid of events that are happening, trust in your Heavenly Mother. I am, My children, preparing you through My messages for My Son's Coming. Be like simple children, dependent on their mother for everything, I am tireless and I am guiding everything.* The world, My children, has gone beyond that for which God has made it. I have been sent into the world to protect you, while the battle is on, so trust yourselves to Me completely and do as your Holy Mother requests and all will go well. Be a constant source of inspiration for one another. I am with you always. Love Me, come to Me, long for Me, comfort Me, My heart yearns for My beloved little children to console Me. I love you more than you can ever comprehend. My love knows no bounds. I, My children, long for you always. (Here I feel Our Lady's love and longing and sadness. I feel so sorry for Her, She is so beautiful I believe we would die if we knew how much She loves us.) **My children, God is coming soon** (I feel a tremendous

* *"Guiding everything": as Queen of Heaven and earth, and as merciful Mother of us all, but always under God and in complete conformity to His will. This is not an infinite love, such as God's love is, but it means that Our Lady loves us to the utmost of Her ability, or completely in so far as She is able.*

urgency in Her voice); **help Me to bring more children to Him. Quickly, I tell you, do all you can and more. I love you and bless you, each one of you. Pray, pray, pray! Go in peace."**

78.

Suffer for souls

9 February 1993 *Tuesday*

Holy Mother:

"My dearest child, so dear to Me. Continue on the path I have marked out for you. You are going to suffer much for souls, so do not be surprised when they abandon you or ridicule you or reject you. This is My hour, and I along with you, My child, suffer also. You console Me greatly by your prayers and sacrifices. Do not be sad. You know what awaits you. I love you, I am beside you now as you write. I love you, remain docile and humble. But always proclaim My Son. When necessary, wherever you see wrong, right it. Rest now."

79.

I will not abandon you

9 February 1993 *Tuesday*

Holy Mother:

"My dear child, I am beside you at present. I am helping you, do not fear, I will pray to My Divine Son for the grace of a stronger faith, to withstand the sorrows of this time. Unite yourself to Me, I will not abandon you, give your sorrow to Me and together we will suffer for souls."

80.

Be humble

9 February 1993 *Tuesday*

Holy Mother:

"My child, you must be careful never to boast, always remember to be humble."

81.

I see you in great danger

15 February 1993 *Monday 2.00 pm*

Holy Mother:

"My child, write, down on your knees in thanksgiving for the graces given to you by God. Do not be fearful as the pagans are when they worry or fear as this comes from the Evil One, do as My Son said. Trust in Me and know that you have a Mother who loves you very much.

Daughter, time is so short, be prepared much more, My Son is coming very soon before even the elect realize. I need your prayers and consolation. Heaven, My child, is shocked at the atrocities that are occurring in the world, I fear for My lost children, pray, pray, pray (here I feel great distress and sorrow as She is pleading with us for prayer), **I love you and I pray unceasingly for you to My Son to give you the graces necessary to carry out this mission, as I see you in great danger, because the Evil One will try to deceive you in many ways. This is why I need to be closer to you now more than ever. So take My hand and do not fear, as long as you do as I say, I will be consoled. Praise God in Heaven and the Angels and Saints await your prayers and requests as always, pray to them and they will assist you greatly. I pray that God's will be done. Go to Mass more often, be in My Son's Heart and there you will receive more graces and strength. Go in peace!"**

82.

Jesus wants us to be united to Him in every situation

February 1993

Jesus:

These last few days, November 1995, many experiences of my past and dreams came flooding back to me. One was of one morning I did not go to Mass and I was at home rushing through my housework as I had a lot to do that day. When suddenly, while I was washing dishes at the sink, I became aware of Jesus on my right hand side. At first I got a shock and I felt the hair stand up on the back of my neck with fright. Also I felt guilty as I had not received Him that day (in Holy Communion). Yet what came from Him was great love. He was serene, gentle and kind. He was not judgemental. Again He reminded me of a long lost brother who had not seen you in a long time and loved you very much and was delighted to see you. Jesus said, **"Geraldine, you did not come to visit Me today, I missed you."** He let me know how much He longs to be with us and He said to me, **"When you are doing your housework, or whatever you do, always be united to Me: Talk to Me, I am with you."** Now I know Jesus loves us so much that He wants us to be united to Him in every situation and to be conscious of Him and His presence throughout the day.

83.

Go multiply My Cenacles everywhere

18 February 1993 *Thursday*

Holy Mother:

"My dearest child, consoler of My heart, thank you for your prayers and sacrifices. Do not be afraid, I will be with you even in the darkest moments. Trust Me more, My dear little one. Offer all to My Son who loves you so dearly. I wish for you to remain faithful to Me always,

I Myself will be waiting to place a crown on your head for the work that you do for My Son. Go, My child, and multiply My Cenacles* everywhere, I will guide and protect you always."

84.

Suffer for souls

8 March 1993 *Monday* *St. John of God Optional Memorial*

Holy Mother:

"My child, it is My desire that you pray, fast, and live My messages. I am at present beside you. I am always assisting by your side. I rejoice when you confide to Me the sorrows of your heart. I am happiest when I am close to My children. Today, My child, I am happy. I am happy because many of My straying children have cried out to Me to help them and I rejoice when a soul turns back to Me. This is why I long for My chosen children to help Me save souls. My Son does not want your condemnation. Pray more and suffer for souls. Tell My son."**

85.

Adore the Blessed Sacrament

18 March 1993 *Thursday* *Lenten Week Day St. Cyril of Jerusalem Optional Memorial*

Holy Mother:

"I will be happy to see My children praying in My Son's house and adoring Him in the Blessed Sacrament."

---

* *A Cenacle is a gathering for Christian prayer. Two or three are enough to form a Cenacle.*

** *"Son" meaning Spiritual Director.*

86.

Pray hearts will be touched and opened

18 March 1993 Thursday 6.00 pm St. Cyril of Jerusalem Optional Memorial

Holy Mother:

"My child, be at peace, God is guiding everything. Do not worry or be concerned, I will permit whatever happens. I wish you to give the messages to the magazine, because this is another door which My Son has opened for you. Pray that many hearts will be touched and opened. Praise and thank My Divine Son for those favours in which you have been allowed to participate. I bless you in the name of the Father and of the Son and of the Holy Spirit."

87.

I will help you

25 March 1993 Thursday Annunciation of the Lord Solemnity

Holy Mother:

"My child, your pain is from the Most High.* He wishes to use your suffering to appease His anger. Do not worry, I will help you."

* *I was having a lot of pain and was taking lots of painkillers, but they were not working. So Holy Mother said, your pain is from God, no painkillers will take it away.*

88.

The more worthless the sinner, the greater is My mercy

3 April 1993 *Saturday 9.00 pm, First Saturday in Lent*

Jesus:

"I have chosen you among many not because you are more worthy but because it is My Father's wish that through you I will bring more souls to My Divine Mercy. It pleases Me very much when you pray more because it is then that I can confide to you the secrets of My Sacred Heart. I wish to make known to souls how great My mercy is, the more worthless the sinner the greater is My mercy. I wish you to pray continuously to My Divine Heart and there you will find all the strength you need to continue your journey to Me. Be joyful and confident in your sufferings. Offer them to Me and I will bless you for this."

89.

The Grace of God will sustain you

6 April 1993 *Tuesday* *Tuesday of Holy Week*

Holy Mother:

"Tell My child ...., 'Jesus will bless your family abundantly, because you have seen fit to do His Holy Will. Do not worry, My child, do you think I would abandon you and your family in your need? No, My child, the grace of My Son will sustain you both. Fear not, rejoice in your decision, as it is so necessary for the salvation of the world that My children respond to My call. Your mother will be especially blessed on this trip as Jesus will touch her heart. Your children will not leave My arms in your absence. Do not distress yourself, I will provide everything. Jesus blesses you. Go in peace.' "

90.

My mercy is running out and My justice will soon be known

10 April 1993 *Saturday* *Holy Saturday*

Holy Week, after a painful morning in prayer

Jesus:

"My mercy is running out and My justice will be known. Come before the Blessed Sacrament. Do not delay any more as I will take this into account later on. Too many souls are being lost and you may have to give an account to Me of those who may have been saved."

91.

Make amends for the indifference shown to Me in the Blessed Sacrament

10 April 1993 *Saturday* *Holy Saturday*

Jesus:

"My children, faithful followers of My Mother, I give you My special blessing in this Holy Week. Children, listen, your Father* speaks. I wish you to make amends for the indifference shown Me in the Blessed Sacrament. Prepare more before for those who do not. Fast, especially now in the time of My Passion. Do not worry, I will help. Implore My mercy for sinners. Make up for all I am suffering and appease My anger. I bless you and the Holy Trinity blesses you. Be at peace."

* *"Father," if a Priest can rightly be called "the father" of one's soul, how much more can Jesus? (cf. 1 Cor. 4:15, St. Paul as "father")*

92.

Sacrifice and penance

12 April 1993 *Monday* *Easter Monday*

Holy Mother:

"I am rejoicing in his work. And not to worry, I am guiding everything, as My Son wishes to use him in the area and his mission is to spread devotion to Me and My Son. Tell him I am very close to him and I see all that happens. The sorrow of My heart is immense and I need much prayer, sacrifices and penance. I delight in his devotion to Me and I bless him. In the name of the Father, and of the Son and of the Holy Spirit. Go in peace to love and serve the Lord."

93.

Humble yourself

12 April 1993 *Monday 2.00 pm* *Easter Monday*

Holy Mother:

"Yes, My daughter, humble yourself before Me, for I am meek and humble at heart. My daughter, I wish all My children be united in prayer, as you cannot begin to comprehend the evil that surrounds you. Arm yourselves in My Holy Rosary. Be humble and obedient towards one another and remember whoever is first will be last and whosoever is last will be first. Be confident in all your afflictions, as your redemption is at hand. I wish to make known the sufferings of My Immaculate Heart. Pray for peace."

94.

Seek only the Kingdom of God

13 April 1993 *Tuesday* *Easter Tuesday*

Holy Mother:

"My dear child, I thank you for your prayers and sacrifices. Tell My chosen ones (those about to go on a pilgrimage), **My Son has called them on this pilgrimage to do His Holy Will, that is, to do a special work for God. This work will be blessed abundantly by the Holy Spirit. It gives Me great joy to see you come in such great numbers. Fear not, I am guiding everything. Jesus, My Divine Son, has a mission for each and everyone who comes with an open heart! When the faithful are in adoration He will bestow an abundance of blessings and graces on all present. Many will receive divine gifts to help continue the work My Son has prepared for them. Do not, My children, come asking for many things, seek only the Kingdom of God, and the rest will be given in abundance.* Do everything with love, My children, supporting one another and rejoicing in My Son. Go in peace, My children, to love and serve the Lord, from whom all good things come."**

95.

My Immaculate Heart will triumph

16 April 1993 *Friday 2.00 pm* *Friday after Easter*

Holy Mother:

"My daughter, I wish to make known that My Immaculate Heart will triumph. Pray, fast and do much penance as there is not much time left, do not worry but cling to Me in all your troubles. Come, My children, and

* *She wanted us to ask for an outpouring of the Holy Spirit. If we do this, the rest is given in abundance because the Holy Spirit knows exactly what we need. God cannot really reach us on that superficial level if we come seeking only for things. She did not want us to come only seeking answers to problems, She wanted us to desire to come closer to God, and God would generously take care of our other needs.*

console your Mother who loves you so much. Come and repent, forgive all offences and cease to offend Jesus."

96.

For protection against the Evil One

24 April 1993 *Saturday* *St. Fidelis of Sigmaringen Optional Memorial*

Holy Mother:

"Tell My daughter ....: 'I love you, be not afraid, I will help you. The Evil One wishes to destroy your family. Do not let him, fight back with love and prayer. I am praying, My child, every day for you. I give you My signs all around you to console you. You are blessed, My daughter, and in spite of your wretchedness I love you. Go to Confession and the Sacraments more now. You will need them to survive. Do not worry, pray to the Saints for the gifts of Fortitude, Patience and Perseverance. Offer all and unite your pain to Mine and together we will suffer for souls. I love you, My child. The Evil One wishes to destroy you and your family. Love them, comfort them, pray for them. I will do the rest. God bless you, go in peace.' "

97.

Jesus rejoices in adoration

24 April 1993 *Saturday* *St. Fidelis of Sigmaringen Optional Memorial*

Medjugorje

Adoration of the Blessed Sacrament between 10.00 and 11.00 pm. This was probably the most beautiful moment in Medjugorje. It was night time with only the candles burning, everyone was kneeling. Jesus was present in the Blessed Sacrament, exposed, and two Priests were saying spontaneous acts of love to Jesus, while kneeling at the altar. Then we began to sing

a beautiful hymn in a low voice – “Jesus Remember Me” (this was the first time I had heard this Taizé hymn). The feeling was Heavenly. Beside me I see a man clearly with great devotion, rosary beads around his neck, his face to the floor, singing with so much love and fervour. Such love! I was very moved as I watched his children watch him and I thought, Jesus, how wonderful it would be if others had faith like this and wishing all my heart that this could be so. I clearly heard Jesus say, **“Ah yes, but if this were so, what would you have to offer Me,”** and I realized how precious our suffering is to Him when offered. Praise be to Jesus. Then, as I began to pray the Our Father, Hail Mary, etc., I found that I was praying from the heart, each word had so much meaning and I really felt as though I was talking to God. I realized the more I prayed like this, the closer I seemed to be coming to God and the more joy I was feeling. I felt wonderful, I remembered then, when Our Lady said, prayer will be a joy for you.

Then I saw Jesus standing in front of the altar dressed in a white robe. He was looking at everyone. I was looking at Him from where I was, then as if I was either standing behind Him or seeing through His eyes, I am not sure, I could see all the people in front of me worshipping and adoring Him and I could feel His love flowing towards all these people. He was looking at them with such joy and so much love, clearly moved beyond words, as if there was no greater gift we could give Him, and His happiness and joy was breathtaking. I realized how much He loves and delights in us adoring Him. Then this scene passes and again, back in my seat, I am looking up at the altar and this time a little boy appears on a throne. I recognize Him as the Infant Jesus of Prague. This little boy was sitting on a chair, like a throne, fit for a King. He was about four years old with blond curls to His shoulders and His skin was so clear. He was dressed like the Infant Jesus of Prague. A beautiful little boy, and I was very aware of His majesty. He was so majestic, looking at all the people and smiling at them. Our Lady was on His left and St. Joseph on His right. When this scene passed I was overwhelmed with love, peace and joy, and didn’t want it to end, as I felt I was in ecstasy, and I wanted to hug the first person I saw.

98.

Prayer, penance, reparation and fasting

12 May 1993 *Wednesday, Nereus and Achilleus, Pancras Optional Memorial*

Holy Mother:

"My heart is so sorrowful, console Me, dear child, as I suffer greatly. My Son's wounds have opened and He is in great agony. Defend your Holy Mother in prayer, penance, reparation and fasting. Do not worry what the world thinks of you, as it is passing. Thank you."

99.

Continue to console Me and My Mother

16 May 1993 *Sunday* *Sixth Sunday after Easter*

Holy Mother:

"Tell ...., I bless and rejoice in her work for Me. My dearly beloved Son is longing to comfort and console her in her afflictions. For now she is to offer all to My Merciful Heart and I will bless her abundantly. My child, this is My message: 'Love one another as love covers a multitude of sins. You are in My care.'"

Jesus:

"Dear child, beloved of My heart, how I rejoice in your work for love of Me. Continue to console Me and My Mother. Do not be sad, I am guiding everything. I bless you."

100.

Help Me!

16 May 1993 *Sunday* *Sixth Sunday after Easter*

Prayer Groups of Reparation were started because Holy Mother appeared to me crying, saying, **"Help Me, help Me,"** and begging for reparation because Her Son is already too much offended by blasphemies, etc.

101.

The Evil One will deceive you in many ways

16 May 1993 *Sunday* *Sixth Sunday after Easter*

Holy Mother:

"My daughter, I wish to convey to you My innermost suffering. Satan is waging war on My children in a very vicious way, you must consecrate yourselves to Me and always be mindful of My Motherly protection. My children, the Evil One will deceive you in many ways, stay close to My Maternal Heart and Jesus will help you. The world is in a dreadful state of sin, the battle is worsening. Arm yourselves with the Holy Rosary and receive the Sacrament of Holy Communion often."

102.

Do not be sad

7 June 1993 *Monday* *Tenth Week in Ordinary Time*

Holy Mother:

"My dear child, do not grieve so intensely in your heart, 'S' (a dear friend of mine who died) **was a very**

dear and devoted woman. The prayers, Masses and sacrifices offered during her life will bring her to Heaven. My dear child, let Me console you. Please I beg you, come to My Immaculate Heart and there you will find consolation, do not be too disheartened. The Lord loves you very much, as do I. This suffering, My child, you should offer in union with the Holy Wounds of My Divine Son in reparation for sins in the world, and Jesus will not only bless you for this but it will be to your greater glory in Heaven where your crown awaits you. Do not despair, My daughter, I am here to help you to endure. My graces at this time will help you and your family. I will never abandon you and I rejoice in your motherhood. Do not be sad as I see your heart so grieved, I love you. Let Me comfort and console you and remember the joy that awaits you in Heaven when you all meet again. I am your Holy Mother and I bless you in the name of the Father and the Son and the Holy Spirit. Amen. Go in peace, My child, to love and serve the Lord."

103.

The Holy Spirit will enlighten you

11 June 1993 *Friday 2.00 pm* *St. Barnabas, Apostle Obligatory Memorial*

Jesus to Fr. ....:

"My dear child, tell My son it is My desire that he assist you in this work which I am doing through you, that I will guide him and all he says and does and the Holy Spirit will enlighten him in all matters relating to this work. My Holy Mother rejoices in this and blesses all you do in the name of the Father and of the Son and of the Holy Spirit. Amen."

104.

Fear not

11 June 1993 *Friday* *St. Barnabas, Apostle Obligatory Memorial*

After the Rosary

Holy Mother:

For ....

"My dear son, beloved of My heart, fear not, I am with you in everything and I am guiding you every day closer to Me."

105.

Offer all your sorrows to Me

11 June 1993 *Friday* *St. Barnabas, Apostle Obligatory Memorial*

Holy Mother:

"My dear child, I love you very much and I do not want your condemnation, My Motherly Heart rejoices in you, be not afraid, I am with you and beside you in all things. You fret and worry, My daughter, please trust in My Son and let His will be done. Accept little daily crosses lovingly. I will help you come to Me and there in My Immaculate Heart you will find rest. My daughter, the Evil One is very strong now, you must disarm him with your prayers. My Son rejoices in the work you do for Him, this work will be for your salvation and for that of others. Do not be disheartened. Trust and pray and leave all in My Son's hands and He will not abandon you. Love one another as I have loved you and rejoice in each other because the Lord has seen fit to do good things for you. Offer all your sorrow to Me and I will give you joy even in your sorrow. Go in peace, My child."

106.

Keep Me company

13 June 1993 *Sunday* *Eleventh Sunday of the Year*

(Fatima Day. The 13th of the month. Our Lady appeared on 13th of each month May to October in 1917, to three children.)

Holy Mother woke me up during the night and asked me to keep Her company and say the Rosary, so I did.

Jesus:

Afterwards I felt Jesus' presence so much I cried for ages with joy. He consoled and comforted me with words like, "My beloved" or, "Beloved of My heart," and told me when I suffer He will always be my strength and I felt Him so close to me His love consumed me. His words filled my heart with such joy, I almost could not bear it. I longed for Him, to be with Him in Heaven. He is so compassionate, loving and understanding, and so wonderful there is no joy to compare with it. I felt like I would die to be parted from Him. I told Him I would suffer anything for Him and I meant it. He assured me He could never let me go during trials and spoke such beautiful things to me, I thought my heart would burst with joy. Jesus, my love, my life, I love You, adore You, worship You, You are my everything.

I praise You with all my heart, soul, mind and body. No words could ever describe what passed between us. It is the ultimate feeling of love and more.

107.

Console your Holy Mother

13 June 1993 *Sunday* *Eleventh Sunday of the Year*

Jesus:

"My child, the pain you received in your heart is like the pain in My heart as I see My children waste their lives in front of the television. (This refers to spending a lot of time in front of the television, and wasting time. I had a sudden pain, like a knife through my heart.)

Write, My child, for souls, it is My desire and My Blessed Mother's desire that the children of the world listen to Our messages given to chosen souls for the salvation of the world. The world is in a dreadful state of decay and I suffer greatly as I see so much sin, injustice, poverty, bloodshed and lack of love among My people, even the elect. Console Me, My children, and suffer with Me in this My hour of Gethsemane. Be not afraid of the evil that surrounds you in the world for only I, the Son of God, can bring you to the Eternal Father. I desire that you forgive all offences and love one another as I have loved you. Be close to My dearly beloved Mother as I have given Her to you as your Mother. Be always close to Her, console Her often as She suffers greatly for souls. Be of good cheer and console each other in your sufferings, I am close to all of you in these difficult times. Pray much for the sins in the world and be a light for all who walk in darkness. The abyss is open now and the smoke of the Evil One has entered into the holiest of places. Pray much, offer all to Me and I will deliver you from the chastisement that will come upon the world soon. I, the Lord your God have spoken, do not be deceived, I will consume the wicked with My presence and the just shall feel My Divine Love. I desire all to listen and to be obedient to My call.

I bless you in the name of the Father and of the Son and of the Holy Spirit. Go in peace to love and serve the Lord."

108.

The Holy Spirit can do many things in your life to help you

14 June 1993 *Monday*

Holy Mother:

"My dear child, today I suffer greatly in My heart as I see so many of My children drifting away. Tell My children I long to be close to them and how it comforts Me when you pray and keep Me company. My children, I fear for My little ones. You are like lambs among wolves. Seek refuge in My Immaculate Heart so that I may guide and protect you. The Holy Spirit can do many things in your life to help you. Invoke Him often, as He is My Spouse too (as well as St. Joseph), **and loves you also. St. Michael has special powers too to help and intercede for you in these difficult times. I bless you in the name of the Father and of the Son and of the Holy Spirit. Amen."**

109.

Forgive all offenders

14 June 1993 *Monday*

Jesus:

"Do not be disheartened, all will be well. Do not let your heart be heavy, My yoke is light. Forgive all offenders and yield not to evil. Pray always to give you strength against the Evil One, I will send you what you need to help you through. Be not afraid and remember, I am with you always. Yield to My will and My heart will rejoice. Pray."

110.

My tears are falling upon you

16 June 1993 *Wednesday 12.00 pm*

Geraldine: *"Oh Blessed Mother, You look so terribly sad and You look like You are suffering."*

Holy Mother:

"My child, it is I, do not fear. I have come to ask you to help Me. I am in great need of your prayers. I cannot express to you enough how sorrowful My heart is, as I watch so many of My children suffer, please console Me. (Here I feel Her sorrow and I am crying.) **My tears are falling upon you, tell all My children I pray continuously for you to My Son, who is so greatly offended by the sins of the world. You must listen, dear children, the justice and wrath of God is about to strike. I cannot hold His arm much longer. Satan is so strong now and wants to destroy you, cling tightly, My children, and let your Mother defend you, love one another as love covers many offences. Pray for your Priests, My sons, for whom I suffer greatly. Do not offend My Son any more, rather make sacrifices and do much penance in reparation. My children, I am close to you always, do not despair, I receive your sacrifices with great joy. Pray always to keep yourselves safe from the Evil One."**

111.

Be prepared

16 June 1993 *Wednesday*

Jesus:

"Let it be known, that I, the Son of God, am coming soon, very soon. Be prepared one and all to meet your Redeemer. For I, your Lord and God, have commanded that you love one another as I have loved you. Be not afraid. Ask for My mercy and it will be given. But My justice is at hand

and I will punish severely the evil ones who refuse to obey Me. I, the Lord your God, have spoken. Let it be known!"

I asked Holy Mother, *"How do I know it's from You?"*

Our Lady says, **"How do you know if a message is from God is if it bears good fruit."**

Our Blessed Mother or Jesus will not give any messages while a television is on. She will only speak in silence or prayer.

112.

Write down what I say, it is important

3 July 1993 *Saturday* *Feast of St. Thomas, Apostle*

Holy Mother:

"My daughter, in spite of your sins, I still love you, do not be discouraged, all will be well. Be kind and loving towards everyone and I will bless you for this. Write down what I say, it is important."

113.

I am greatly saddened by the world

5 August 1993 *Thursday* *Dedication of the Basilica of St. Mary Major Optional Memorial*

Holy Mother:

"My dear child, write down what I say as it is so important. Tell My beloved son .... I take great delight in his mission. In this work he will glorify My Divine Son. He will suffer much in life for love of Me, but to take heart, the merciful love of the Infant Jesus will sustain him. I walk by his side and I guide his every move. I, My daughter, am greatly saddened by the world, it goes closer and closer

towards its ruin. So I need the help of My chosen children who will love and serve Me and My Son. Tell My son, I will help and protect him and I will not abandon him in his afflictions. This son of Mine is precious to My heart and truly courageous. He will assist you greatly in many ways.

Tell My son .... to discern all I have said and to assist you in your mission and to act accordingly."

114.

To a Priest leaving his ministry

6 August 1993 *Friday* *The Transfiguration of the Lord, Feast*

Holy Mother:

"My son, it is I, your Holy Mother. My son, I have come to tell you of My sorrow at your decision, and My Son's sorrow. Please reconsider, and pray a great deal on this matter. Did not My Son call you to this vocation? Why then would He call you to another? Please be guided by Me, do not let earthly pleasures influence your decision. I love you, and My Son takes the greatest delight in your Holy Priesthood. My Adversary is only too happy to accommodate you in any way he can, to entice you. Be, My son, mindful of My presence when you make this announcement and the sorrow with which you wound My heart. I pray for you, My son, before the Father, to give you strength and courage in this present situation and Angels and Saints will pray for you, if you call on them. I bless you and the Holy Trinity blesses you. Go in peace."

115.

The presence of Jesus and Mary

23 August 1993 *Monday* *St. Rose of Lima*
Optional Memorial

Jesus:

"Spiritually, you will be more aware of My presence in the future. Whenever the faithful honour Me or My Mother, We are always there with them."

Geraldine: *"Lord, were You there* (meaning at a prayer meeting)*?"*

And He said, **"Yes, I was there."**

116.

Do not judge

2 September 1993 *Thursday*

Many times Jesus, Holy Mother and I talk about many things and I ask advice and They tell me how best to handle every situation. Once I was talking to some people about Our Lady's appearances around the world, and they snapped at me and said, "It's only important to receive Jesus, not to listen to any people talking about Our Lady." I was hurt and so I went before the Blessed Sacrament and cried to Jesus. *"Why?"* He said, **"Hold your head high, My child, because as you have proclaimed Me, so too will I proclaim you to My Father in Heaven, do not judge, pray for them."** Holy Mother also said firmly, **"Do not judge, only pray for them."** I felt it hurts Our Lady when we judge people.

117.

Go to Mass more and all will go well with you

4 September 1993 *First Saturday 8.15 pm*

Holy Mother:

"My dear child, thank you for your prayers, I need them so much, please try to pray more often and you will see a difference in your life. Dear child, be on your guard, Satan is very strong and wants to destroy you. Be guided by Me, be at peace and pray always to be delivered from evil. My child, you have My protection, I will not let any harm come to you. Jesus will console your heart. Be joyful in all your troubles and let the world see the peace Jesus sends you. You will have more to suffer, dear child, but please do not be upset, you have My promise I will give you special graces during those times to sustain you. Offer it all with a good heart because the reward is great, My child. Come with Me and I will gladden your heart. I will sustain you in the face of opposition, pray more, go to Mass and all will go well with you; be patient, kind and understanding. Wait for God to act and He surely will soon, fear not but rejoice in the Lord, He is merciful."

118.

Honour My Son more in prayer

7 September 1993 *Tuesday Night*

Holy Mother:

"My dear child, write down what I tell you, so it may comfort you later on. My child, as I look upon you from above, I am filled with sadness. My heart longs to console you in your grief. I hurt when you hurt, offer it to Me. My child, put your life in My Son's hands, offer your life to Him to do what He wishes. Then He will surely act in good time, do not worry, trust and pray and live My messages. My child, I want you to honour My Son more in

prayer. Do not worry about your cousins.* They will have My protection during this time, I will sustain them."

119.

Seek only to glorify Him

14 September 1993 Tuesday 6.30 pm, Feast of Triumph of the Cross

Holy Mother:

"Dear daughter, I have let you work together with these Priest sons of Mine, so that God's will may be done."

Geraldine: *"Holy Mother, they are so holy, why can't You speak to them Yourself?"*

Holy Mother: **"Because, My child, My Son goes to the lowest of My children and you fit this description very well."** (She said this with a lot of love and very gently.)

Geraldine: *"Holy Mother, that hurts."* **

Holy Mother: **"My daughter, you should delight in being the littlest because when we think we are better than anyone else, we fall into the sin of pride and we seek to glorify ourselves and not God. So we must rejoice in being nothing as we are all nothing without My Son, and we should praise and thank Him continuously for His goodness and seek only to glorify Him."**

120.

A treasure

15 September 1993 Wednesday Memorial of Our Lady of Sorrows

A dream

Today I had a dream that Jesus appeared on my right hand side with a book opened wide. He said, **"Geraldine, write**

---

* *I was worried about my cousins, who were going through a difficult time.*

** *It seemed a strange thing to say to me as I did not yet understand about humility. I was really appealing to Our Lady to explain what She meant.*

in this book." In the book there was already writing in gold print, and it seemed to signify that the words were more precious than gold. I said, *"Yes, Lord, in a moment,"* and this went on for a while and I kept putting it off, until I eventually woke up realizing I still had not written in this book. Bothered by this all day, I prayed to Holy Mother and She said, **"When Jesus speaks, His words are a treasure. When you do not write it down, this treasure is lost forever and your gift may not last forever, so when you write down everything He says, you have something that WILL last forever and WILL be very precious."**

121.

Speak to the Saints

28 September 1993 *Tuesday 5.15 pm* *St. Wenceslaus Optional Memorial*

Holy Mother:

"My dear child, it is I, do not worry. I am here to guide and look after you. My child, there are many things the Lord wishes you to do for Him. For this you will need constant supervision and guidance. Ask .... to assist you in your journey to My Son. My daughter, Jesus wishes to use you in His plan of salvation for the world, so it is important that you be guided in everything. Much suffering is ahead of you now. But rejoice, I tell you, as you have found great favour with My Son, in spite of your misery, so learn to be joyful in all your troubles and afflictions. The Saints, My child, are very close to you and long to converse with you. Speak to them as you do to Me, and ask for their help in all things. I love you and bless you. Go in peace, My child."

122.

Suffer for love of Me

1 October 1993 *First Friday* *St. Theresa of Child Jesus Memorial*

Holy Mother:

“My daughter, My Son Jesus wishes to speak with you.”

Jesus:

“My dearest Geraldine, beloved of My heart. How I rejoiced in tonight.* Thank you, My daughter, and tell everyone I was present. I am always present when the faithful are in adoration.

Daughter, I wish to convey to you My heart’s desire. I am not happy with the people who do not honour Me and My Holy Mother. I wish you to make amends for all I suffer. Do you wish to accept some suffering for love of Me, as I long to be consoled?”

Geraldine: *“Yes, Lord, I accept whatever Your will is. Forgive me if I too have hurt You.”*

“My beloved, tell My children it is through them I will save the world, through those who continually co-operate and console Me. There is much work to be done, I need only your will in all I ask. The rest I will do Myself. Abandon yourself to Me completely. Rest in Me, I desire this. I long to rest in hearts that are like Mine. Be not afraid of anyone, I am God from whom all good things come. I will judge the living and the dead.”

---

* *There had been a lot of people praying.*

123.

I wish to be adored more in the Blessed Sacrament

3 October 1993 *Twenty-Seventh Sunday in Ordinary Time*

Jesus:

"Tell .... I love him dearly and I delight in his work. I am guiding him in everything. Tell him I wish to be adored more in the Blessed Sacrament and I rejoice in this so much, I give the most graces and blessings at this time. Tell him to bring My flock closer to My Sacred Heart through the Immaculate Heart of My Mother. I rejoice in this. My Mother is so sad and suffers greatly. Help Her more to spread devotion to Me. I need only your co-operation in this."

124.

Look what your sufferings and prayers have done

3 October 1993 *Sunday Morning* *Twenty-Seventh Sunday of the Year*

Dear Diary,

Last night was one of the worst nights of my life. I will try to explain it as best as I can. I am still a little shaky from my experience, I felt I did battle with Satan all night. I will explain as follows: I went into my daughter's bedroom after I heard her moving a lot; I had been awake praying the Rosary, because I had felt the need. It was 1.30 am. I tucked her in and comforted her and tried to get her to go to sleep. Then I left her. But soon after she came to my room and said, "Mum, I can't sleep, I keep having nightmares," and she was very frightened. So I got some holy water and blessed her and put a scapular and medal on her for protection, which left me with no medals on, so I blessed myself. Then I must have dropped off to sleep and I dreamt that Satan

had taken possession of me and was trying to get me to hurt myself.

In the dream I kept telling my husband and son to keep away as I felt this terrifying evil presence inside me trying to get me to kill myself. The feeling was so strong it took everything I had not to take my life. I was so terrified by this presence, that I woke up with fright. Then I realized this evil presence which I had felt was all around me in this room. In my spirit I would see Satan leering at me. (Not with the eyes of the body, but I could see him very clearly. Not in the mind but in front of me with the eyes of the soul.) The form he took was hideous and evil. He laughed at me, and leered at me with hate, "I'll kill you! Get out, you are going to die" and he swore at me. I felt all his evil spirits around me and I was petrified. His voice put the most terrifying fear into me. I have never known fear like it, or hate like it. He despised me and I felt my life was in danger. (And at one point I saw the imprint of Satan's hand on the ceiling with the fingers shaped like a claw.)

At this point, I almost wished I could not see with my spiritual eyes, because I did not want to see him or hear him. I begged Jesus and Holy Mother to help me and all the Angels and Saints too, every Saint I could think of by name I begged for help, but it was as though no one could hear me as nothing happened. I just kept praying through my fear, as I could hear him laughing and calling me names, and just when I felt I was going to die of fear, or I could not take it anymore, I began to feel this presence on my left side, it was St. Michael. I could feel this courage (supernatural) from inside, and my fear was leaving me and I could feel a shield of protection all around me. I could see Satan shrinking away, saying, "Oh, no!," as though he was losing power over me and he was mad.

Then I said, "Get thee behind me, Satan," and I invoked the protection of the Precious Blood of Christ on me and everyone in the house and the house too. I rebuked him in the name of Jesus. I told him, the more he frightened or hurt me, the more I would offer it for the conversion of sinners on earth, for the souls in Purgatory and in reparation, and I realized this is what I had been doing all along, and the more I praised and thanked Jesus for this suffering, even when I felt sure He had abandoned me, the more I could see Satan losing power as though I was

hurting him more. Then Satan disappeared and all his evil spirits and I felt this tremendous peace.

Holy Mother:

Next, Our Lady appeared beside me on my right side, St. Michael was on my left and I saw Our Blessed Mother as I have never seen Her before, dressed in gold and almost breathless as though She had been running, but instead She was breathless with excitement. She kept kissing my cheeks and leaning over me, like a mother bending down to kiss her child goodnight. She seemed to be overcome with joy and said, **"Thank you, thank you, My child. Look, look!"** She said, **"See what your sufferings and prayers have done."** I saw as She showed me many people rising up out of Purgatory to Heaven (I actually saw full length bodies* of men and women flying up through the air to Heaven). I felt Our Lady's anxiousness, as though she was so relieved because the suffering of these souls was over. So now I understood why She was breathless with excitement: it was at seeing so many of Her children go to Heaven. I felt that I had been able to help in their release, and relieved that this frightening experience was over. Now I felt so peaceful all night and went to sleep although it was almost morning. This evil presence lasted for what seemed like hours, before St. Michael came to help me. But now I understood the value of suffering offered.

When I got up I could hardly move. I was sore and exhausted. I felt so much in need of other's prayers..

125.

Prepare to do battle

7 October 1993 *Thursday* *Feast of Our Lady of the Rosary*

Holy Mother:

"My dear child, tell My Priest sons I am calling them together to prepare to do battle. The Church and the world are about to be thrown into great turmoil. Pray

* *These "bodies" represent the souls which are invisible. There are no bodies in Purgatory, only souls.*

very much for the Holy Father, as He suffers greatly for the sins of humanity and is very distressed. He needs your constant support in prayer. Tell My sons I have chosen you to give these messages, which is the holy will of My Son. Prepare humanity now for the greatest battle since time began, which is about to begin. If you do not heed My warnings you will not survive the terrible and evil time ahead; torrents of rain, hail, thunder, earthquakes, catastrophes, natural disasters, murders, corruption, incest, immorality, abortions, Priests and Religious losing faith and committing sacrileges against the Holy Name of My Son, these are taking place. How much more can He take? He is daily crucified, help Me please. I cannot hold back the justice of My Son any more. Please, My sons, prepare now as never before. I am gathering you now from the four corners of the earth to do battle; put on the armour of God* daily and take up your cross and carry it with joy. Go in peace."

126.

Forgive all offences

8 October 1993 *Friday*

Holy Mother:

For ....

"My dearest child, so dear to My heart. I love you more than words can express, do not be sad, My daughter. Jesus, My Son, is guiding everything. Place your heart in Our hearts and there you will find peace, comfort and consolation. My child, My Motherly Heart bleeds in sorrow because of the sins committed. Help Me, My child, pray more, forgive all offences and offer them to Jesus and He will bless you and your family. Do not worry about your father, I have him in My care. Be of good cheer because Jesus loves you and has designs on you and blesses you in all that you do. Go in peace to love and serve the Lord."

---

* *"The armour of God": see Ephesians 6:10 to 17*

127.

Make constant reparation and sacrifices

9 October 1993 Saturday Sts. Denis and Companions or St. John Leonardi Optional Memorial

Holy Mother:

"Dear daughter, write for souls. My dear child, you must act very quickly, time is of the essence. The world, My daughter, is slowly going towards the abyss. Quickly, I tell you, arm yourselves with My Holy Rosary, and the Sacraments, quickly. I cannot stress enough what awaits you, My heart is breaking, help Me please, I cannot hold My Son's hand any longer, He is already too much offended.

Oh, My child, you must tell My Priest sons to prepare now before the just anger of My Son comes upon the world, I cannot bear to think of it, I beg you to listen to Me, I love you and I do not want your condemnation. Pray, pray, pray and beg for God's mercy to sustain you, pray to the Saints to help and guide you. Tell My sons I wish them to make constant reparation and sacrifices to My Divine Son so that the just anger of the Father will be appeased. Tell all My children to come back to Me and to consecrate themselves to the Sacred Heart of Jesus through the Immaculate Heart of Mary. Protect yourselves daily, put on the armour of God* and receive the Sacraments daily. Dear daughter, this mission has been given to you by God, this is why He allowed you to see His anger. (Referring to a previous vision in which Jesus was about to punish the world, about seven years ago.) **Your very souls depend on whether you are faithful to His graces, do not worry, I will assist you in everything. Go in peace."**

---

* *Ephesians 6:10-17*

128.

Emmanuel

13 October 1993 *Wednesday 2.00 pm*

Jesus:

"I am the light of the world, he who believes in Me shall never die. I am Emmanuel."

129.

Do not be sad

October 1993

Holy Mother:

"God the Father wishes to use you in His work for the salvation of the world. Do not be sad, I am with you in all things. Satan will not harm or defeat you, call on and look to Me, I will not abandon you. Pray much, do not be afraid or disheartened, the coming chastisement can be lessened by prayer, pray for deliverance. Tell My Priest sons I love and protect them. Tell .... My heart delights in his mission, the grace of God is with him and I shall assist him in all his necessities. Go in peace."

130.

Say the Divine Mercy Chaplet in reparation for sinners

15 October 1993 *Friday* *St. Theresa of Avila Memorial*

Holy Mother:

To ....

"I love you, do not be afraid, I am with you in everything. Pray to My Son, Jesus in atonement for the sins in the world and in reparation for sinners. Say the Divine Mercy

Chaplet. Do not be discouraged, I will intercede for you to My Divine Son. Be patient and trust and accept My Son's Will when it is shown to you. Pray, fast, and live My messages. Go in peace."**

131.

They reject My teaching

30 October 1993 Saturday

Jesus:

"My dear child, let it be known to one and all that I, Jesus, am terribly offended by mankind. They reject My Teaching and Love, and My Father is about to punish them for their sins. You will have much to suffer, daughter, but the anger of My Father is just. The whole earth will tremble in fear when I come. Make no mistake. I am coming soon to judge one and all. My child, I have chosen you from among many, not because you are worthy, but because I love you and I chose you before time began to bring souls to Me. I will bless you for this abundantly. Rest in My love."

132.

Put your family first

30 October 1993 Saturday

Holy Mother:

"My daughter, I want to tell you how much I love you and am pleased with your willingness to desire to do God's Holy Will. This pleases Him greatly. Continue to pray for this. My child, I am not happy with the continual talking in church in front of My Son. More respect is needed in His presence. And I am very pleased to be honoured under the title of 'Our Lady of Fatima', as it is vital to the present age. More Prayer Groups should be formed under this title.

Dear daughter, put your family first, do not let housework build up, have a daily routine. Pray more for your children.

Dear daughter, evil people* are summoning up spirits to attack God's chosen and consecrated children. I wish you to invoke the Precious Blood of Jesus on them and pray Novenas for them. All God's chosen people will suffer in some way."

133.

Do not despair

3 November 1993 Wednesday 12.00, St. Martin de Porres Optional Memorial

Holy Mother:

"My child, write this down for My child .... Tell her I am with her in everything and I love her very much. My heart grieves for your lost children. Together we will offer our suffering to My Son who is being crucified all over again by this depraved humanity. My daughter, do not despair, I am interceding before My Son for you, pray always to be delivered from the Evil One. I rejoice in your love for Me. I am beside you comforting you as you cry. I bless you in the name of the Father and of the Son and of the Holy Spirit. Amen."

134.

Seek refuge in My Immaculate Heart

5 November 1993 First Friday

Holy Mother:

"My dearest child .... Let My peace descend on you. I wish you to seek refuge in My Immaculate Heart. There you will be consoled. My child, never before as now has My heart been so sorrowful. Through your suffering we are united. Please offer this to Me in reparation for sins in the world and the Lord, your God, will bless you for this.

---

* *Evil people – refers to people at a Satanists' Conference currently being held.*

Dear daughter, the time is coming when all mankind will suffer much. But the joy that awaits you is for all eternity. Let the offering of your life to Me be for the salvation of souls. Pray always. Receive the Sacraments so as to receive graces from My Son."

135.

Persevere, My children

12 November 1993 *Friday 6.00 pm* *St. Josaphat Memorial*

Holy Mother:

"My child, oh how you will suffer for souls, do not be discouraged, I am close to you. Be not afraid, My mantle will protect you, pray always to be delivered. My daughter, My heart bleeds for My chosen children because you are like little lambs among wolves, but the mercy of My Divine Son will sustain you. Do not become disheartened, My children, the great consolation that I receive from you will be to you the utmost joy in Heaven. Persevere, My children, and look towards Heaven in all your trials and Jesus will light the way. Offer all to Me for souls and the greatest joy will be yours. Oh My daughter, how My heart longs for you to be with Me in Paradise. My love for you is fathomless. Console Me, dear children, stay close to Me and My Motherly Heart will console you. My love for you is so great you could never comprehend it. Give My love to everyone you meet, bless everyone and pray more for My lost children. Amen."

136.

Try not to answer back

15 November 1993 *Monday* *Albert the Great Optional Memorial*

Holy Mother:

"**In our sufferings we hold one another up.**" Holy Mother kisses me, holds up my chin and blesses me. She tells me She loves me and says, "**When anyone hurts you, try not to answer back and ask God to have mercy on their soul, forgive them their sins and bring them to everlasting life.**"

137.

Pray more for your children

16 November 1993 *Tuesday* *St. Margaret of Scotland or St. Gertrude Optional Memorial*

Holy Mother:

"**Invoke St. Michael constantly and ask God for mercy. Do not worry about your children. Pray more for them. This is your sanctification and purification. Offer everything no matter how mundane. Tell Jesus your sorrows and hurts, He understands. Ask the Holy Spirit to enlighten you and have recourse to your Angel Guardian who will comfort you. Be at peace. In spite of your sins and difficulties, My Angels are with you. My daughter, be not afraid, I will help you to endure. Daughter, I place My Son in your arms to comfort you** (meaning the Infant Jesus). **Sacrifice everything for Him as He loves you. Console Him more. Love Him more. Adore Him. Worship Him. Offer everything to Him. Praise Him more. He desires this so much from His devoted children and spouses. He longs for us to come to Him more so that we can receive more of His love, which He gives abundantly. Our Father in Heaven watches over you constantly and is pleased with you and your growth. Thank Him for His goodness, His**

greatness, His generosity, patience and His love for you. Offer your heart to Him and He will bring you to holiness. Pray for your brothers and sisters in Christ and wait for God to act.* Go in peace."

138.

Love everyone

16 November 1993 Tuesday St. Margaret of Scotland or St. Gertrude Optional Memorial

Holy Mother:

"**My child, I wish you not to be afraid. I love you.** (Here I cry, because I see Holy Mother lifting up my chin and She looks so beautiful; so full of love and motherly concern for me. Crying, I say, *"Oh Mother, how can I ever repay Jesus for His goodness, which I don't deserve. I am nothing, it is too much."*) **You can repay Him by giving this love, His love, to everyone. Love everyone like this, as He loves you when you don't deserve it. Love others when they don't deserve it and say when they hurt you: 'God, have mercy on them, forgive them their sins and bring them to everlasting life.'** (Then She kisses me, blesses me with the Sign of the Cross on the forehead.) **In our sufferings** (Hers and mine) **we will hold each other up."** I understood this to mean that She comforts me and I comfort Her with prayer.

139.

I give you My strength and courage

17 November 1993 Wednesday St. Elizabeth of Hungary, Memorial

Today is the day .... asked me to talk about my trip to Medjugorje to people at a Prayer Group. I stayed for Expo-

* *To wait patiently for God's grace to work in the people for whom we pray.*

sition of the Blessed Sacrament and Rosary, and Our Lady said to me (because I was feeling nervous), **"Repeat after Me: 'It is not I, but Jesus in me.' "** I did so. She wants us to die to ourselves and let Jesus live in us. Then as I was soon to speak, still feeling a little nervous, I was trying to pray and then I was aware in spirit of going up towards Heaven to God the Father. I found myself looking down towards the earth from a great height, with God the Father Almighty beside me. I had a tremendous awareness of His almighty power, looking over the whole earth and I could see all the people and myself below here on earth, we are like tiny little creatures – like dots or specks, and I was made aware of how little we are in comparison to Almighty God. Then God the Father (He filled me with reverence and awe on such a scale you could not even begin to describe it) said to me with tremendous authority and firmness, **"TELL THEM I AM COMING, AND TO PREPARE."** But this was said with severity so that you immediately wanted to do as He asked because you could feel the importance of this message and would not dare to offend Him as He is almighty. If people did not prepare now and quickly we cannot imagine or comprehend the seriousness of the consequences, and I was filled with a great desire to plead and encourage everyone to quickly do as He asks. We would, I feel, die or fright if we knew what could happen. The Father impressed me as a very just and loving Father. Yet what He asks for is so important that we would bring His wrath on ourselves if we do not do what He wants. He gave me to understand that He is so serious because the salvation of souls is at stake which is the most important thing in His eyes. He wants to save us, not punish us, but it is up to us.

I looked down and I could see everyone in this Prayer Group. God is watching everything, every move, every thought. He is really and truly there with us. Then I opened my eyes and I was back with the Group again, and I saw Jesus in spirit put out His hand and touch my shoulder saying, **"I give you My strength and courage."** Then He disappeared. I felt like jumping up and shouting to everyone, "God is here, He is coming, prepare, prepare. He is coming soon and is watching everything." However, I just gave the talk on my pilgrimage and could not stay afterwards for tea as I had to collect the children from school.

The next morning I was praying and I heard a voice, a man's voice, not Jesus'. He said, **"I am your Guardian Angel, my**

name means 'Forbearance'. Jesus has given you into my care. You have many gifts of which you are not aware. You can speak to the Saints and they can also speak to you. Praise and thank the Lord for His goodness and mercy." At this point I felt I was loosing my mind. I was afraid I was being deceived, but yet I was very excited and at the same time worried that I might be imagining this. So I asked Holy Mother, *"Can this really be happening? How do I know if it is or is not from Satan?"* She said my Spiritual Director would help me discern, and again She asked me to continuously thank Jesus for His goodness.

Then I thought of St. Rita, and I could not get her out of my mind, so I asked Holy Mother if I could speak to her, and She agreed. I waited, there was a pause, and then I heard a woman speak. I was greatly surprised, it was a different, completely different voice to Our Lady's, and I could feel her personality in the same way as I had felt the different personality of the Angel. I am somehow aware of what they are feeling inside. St. Rita referred to me as her sister in Christ. She said that God had allowed her to speak to me, to help me. I told her I had read a little about her and she started to tell me more about her life here on earth. She said she suffered many hard trials. She told me to treat my husband with great respect as God has placed him in authority over me and I would answer to God if I did not. She said to say a Novena for him to the Sacred Heart, and fast, and to pray for my children.

Then I felt this is too much and I asked Holy Mother if I could speak to my patron saint, St. Margaret Mary, to whom Our Lord appeared. This time the feeling was quite different again, another different personality and voice. I felt so much love coming from her for me. She said she knew how much I loved her and assured me that she loved me very much in return and she prayed to Jesus for me, and this is why He has given me this grace. She said, **"I thank you for your love and devotion to me."** Then she said, **"Jesus has great designs on you and He has chosen you as He chose me to help in His plan of Salvation for the world."** She said the closer I came to Jesus or the holier I became the more Jesus will delight my heart. And she said the goodness of the Lord is wonderful and to adore Him for it. She said in the years to come Jesus wanted the Saints to help and assist me in my

mission and trials. She told me they intercede greatly before God for us. Then she said she would speak to me again.

I then said, *"Holy Mother, I am very excited and happy but also amazed and unsure."* After which I prayed the Prayers of Reparation. Then I felt so much love for Jesus that I thought my heart would burst. I felt this way a day later, so excited and happy, at the same time I was worried as I did not want to be deceived. I was afraid I was going mad. Now I also feel so much more love for Jesus, like a spouse, that I wanted to get up to go to 7 am Mass before work. On the days I could not make Mass I wanted to fast. Since then I found fasting so much easier.

140.

Satan is after Consecrated Souls and Priests

18 November 1993 *Thursday* *Dedication of the Churches of the Sts. Peter and Paul, Apostles Optional Memorial*

Holy Mother:

Once when I was worried over something, Holy Mother said, **"Bless yourself five times in honour of My Son's Holy Wounds and repeat after each one, 'Jesus, I love You and I trust in You.' "** After I said it all She said, **"And mean it!"** Then when I did it again meaning every word, I felt graces coming to me, it was like a chanting and it felt very peaceful and relaxing.

Once I had a dream and I dreamt I was in a church praying and two Priests were on my right side praying too, when in front of me, to my terror, I see a huge dragon, he was taller than the church. I see him towering over the church like he possessed it. Then I notice the Priests have gone and I somehow know it is because they are not strong enough to fight. They are overcome by it. Then I try to hide as this dragon is trying to devour me. I am praying all the while and I notice each prayer I say is wounding him like a knife, or a weapon that is hurting him. So I am fighting him with prayer as a weapon. But it is not enough,

he is far too powerful for me, and just as I feel exhausted and think I am about to die, something lifts me up and holds me up under my arms and I am able to fight him much better. When I look to my left and right to see who is holding me up, it is the Angels and Saints.

In the dream the Priests were not able to withstand the onslaught of Satan. I understood that Satan was after Priests and Consecrated Souls in the first place. I felt this dream was of very great importance and I felt the effects of it very much. The next day I felt that this dream was of great significance for the Church and for souls. I was moved to pray very much for Priests as I realized in what great danger they were, and Consecrated Souls as well. Only with the intercession of the Saints and the Angels will they be able to withstand the onslaught of Satan.*

141.

Prayers overcome evil

18 November 1993 *Thursday* *Dedication of the Churches of the Sts. Peter and Paul, Apostles Optional Memorial*

Holy Mother:

"My child, you know how powerful the Evil One is now. He is waging war on you, dear daughter. This is why you need to pray more and earnestly to overcome him. I will help you succeed. He will be allowed to test you, but Jesus will intervene. Your dream (refer 140) **signifies his strength so that you might protect yourself from him. Do not underestimate him and when you feel in despair, call Me, My child. Ask for the intercession of the Saints to help you. My child, you must receive the Sacraments more often, so you can receive more graces. Your Guardian Angel will help you today. My daughter, the grace of God is with you. Fear not, the yoke of Jesus is easy and His burden light. Persevere**

* *So I feel God is showing me, on my own I am no match for Satan, but with the intercession of the Saints and Angels I am much stronger and with their help I will be able to fight Satan, otherwise I would not survive.*

all your troubles and the Lord will bless you abundantly when it is over.

Your grandparents pray for you constantly as do your daughter and sister." (This refers to a sister and daughter who had died years ago.)

142.

Be united to Me in everything

21 November 1993 *Sunday* *Christ the King Solemnity*

Jesus:

At a church, in front of the picture of the Sacred Heart, I was praying in reparation to His heart, when I heard Jesus say, **"Be My Spiritual Spouse."** Now I asked the Lord, *"How?"* and He said, **"Be united to Me in everything and be pure, then I will give you the greatest joy imaginable, in your heart."** My heart took flight and I understood it to mean that there was no greater joy than this on earth. I felt I should immediately go to Confession. Since then, I feel a more intimate closeness with Jesus, beautiful but scary, because I am not worthy of such an honour.

143.

I am God, I can do all things

21 November 1993 *Sunday* *Christ the King Solemnity*

Jesus:

I am in the lounge room reading, when I look up at the Sacred Heart picture of Our Lord, and He comes alive to me and asks me to talk and pray to Him and He wants my undivided attention at this moment. I ask the Lord, *"How is it possible to be Your spiritual spouse and be married to my husband?"* He said, **"I united your husband and you in Holy Matrimony, this is**

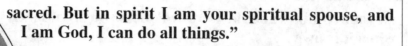

sacred. But in spirit I am your spiritual spouse, and I am God, I can do all things."

144.

Only love Me and carry out My Divine Will

23 November 1993 Tuesday *St. Clement I, Pope, or St. Columban Optional Memorial*

Jesus:

"It is I, Jesus, I am happy you are starting to write more, it is so important for souls. My beloved spouse, how you delight Me. (Here I feel the most overwhelming joy and love, I am crying.) **My dearest one, it is true you are not worthy of Me, but I, Jesus, will make you so. Be not afraid of Me, what I desire most is that you try to love Me as I love you. My heart is overflowing with love and I wish to give it to you. How happy and joyful it makes Me to do this to be united to My spouse in such a way, if only all My children could love Me more, how My heart would delight them. My daughter, I, Jesus, have chosen you to help Me, do not question why, only love Me and carry out My Divine Will. This is all I ask of you and the greatest joy will be yours for all eternity. Seek to console your God, your Divine Master. I, Jesus, am suffering so much. I desire you to love Me to make amends for all I suffer. I have such need of you.** (Here I feel Jesus' pain and sadness.) **My daughter, I take tremendous delight in your heart, there I choose to rest. I delight in you and love you and desire your heart to be in Mine and Mine in yours. Go in peace, I am with you."**

145.

I will judge severely

8 December 1993 *Wednesday* *Immaculate Conception Solemnity*

Jesus:

"Today, My child, I wish to tell you My heart's desire. I desire souls to come to Me and console Me in this hour of great trial. Here they will be restored and renewed. These days preceding My Second Coming are very wicked and I will judge severely. The wicked will perish in My sight. You, My beloved ones, shall receive your crown of glory and will join Angels and Saints. Continue to persevere in all trials, clinging to Me and My Holy Mother. Invoke the Archangels St. Michael, St. Gabriel and St. Raphael, and also the Saints who intercede for you. The great calamity is upon you, and Satan, My Adversary, is pursuing you with all his might and fury, so only your prayers can protect you from him. But trust in Me to deliver you and fear not. In the end My Holy Mother and I will win. For now, I ask obedience to My Sacred Words. Do not disappoint Me, dear little ones, gather together in prayer often and receive My love and power. The road ahead is dark and paved with many thorns, but remember what awaits those who persevere to the end."

146.

Abandon yourself totally

8 December 1993 *Wednesday* *Immaculate Conception Solemnity*

Holy Mother:

"You are still distressed and doubtful. Please, My child, feel My love and abandon yourself totally to Me and trust and believe in what I say. Your prayers have been granted by the Most High and My Son wishes to lift you up. Please receive this peace and pass it on to others. Oh, how

My heart delights in you, My child. Pray for .... and ...., they suffer too, in mind and body. May the grace and peace of My Son be with you always."

147.

Rest in My love

28 December 1993 Tuesday *Feast of the Holy Innocents*

Holy Mother:

"My dear child, do not be worried or discouraged, I am with you in everything. Daughter, I am always with you, rest in My heart. There I will give you all you need. Be not afraid of anyone or anything, I will provide. Daughter, I am happy." She was happy because I was giving more time to prayer and She was able to come back more into my life. **"I will bless you abundantly. Rest in My love and be at peace. Offer all to Me and the Angels will assist you."**

WARNING OF A COMING EVENT

The following two messages are included at this point because of their urgency and importance:

148.

Prepare now

5 April 1995 *Wednesday* *St. Vincent Ferrer Optional Memorial*

God the Father:

"Daughter of the Living Word*, go and prepare humanity for My Son's Second Coming. I am sending a chastisement, the like of which has never been, or will be again. Shout it from the rooftops. Do not be afraid of anyone.

* *Jesus later explains, 3 July 1995:* **'I call you this to remind you that My Word is alive. Read it more.'**

Go and proclaim this message. PREPARE NOW, ATONE, SUFFER, PRAY AND PREPARE."

Here I am commanded by the great justice of God the Father to make reparation and prepare people for a great catastrophe which He is about to send. His tone of voice was commanding, urgent, demanding and full of authority and anger. His warning is stern and He wants us to quickly do as He asks, as we cannot imagine how great the catastrophe will be. I see red all around me. I feel it represents His great justice and wrath. I feel so afraid for humanity as I felt His anger, like a dam ready to break (as if He can't take anymore). I have now the desire to pray, suffer and atone more as He demands it. I feel it would be in my best interest to do so. Even though I am writing this, my words are not capturing the full extent of this experience. I feel like we will suffer more if we don't obey. The more we atone now, the less we will suffer later.

Notes by the Spiritual Director:

The core of the message is that reparation should be made urgently and we should quickly reform our lives. In this way we should always be prepared for God's visitation. We know that God's just punishments can be averted or lessened by conversion, prayer and penance. The principal importance of such a message is to bring about a sincere return to God and to remind us of the urgent necessity of making reparation for sins committed. Fear and alarm in itself is not the response God would want. Here is the response I would suggest:

1. HUMILITY: to humble ourselves before God.
2. TO ASK FOR MERCY.
3. DO WHAT YOU CAN: If you are thinking of doing something and are feeling resentful to the messages, because you feel that what you are called to do is too much, then don't do that, do something less, but do it with love, with as much love as possible. At the same time admitting your weakness and limitations before the Father.
4. SAY AN UNCONDITIONAL 'YES' TO THE FATHER: asking that He be merciful, throwing oneself onto God's mercy.

149.

Wake up from your slumber

26 December 1995 *Tuesday 4.30 pm, Feast of St. Stephen, First Martyr*

Jesus:

"This New Year (1996) **brings you ever closer to My chastisement*. Wake up, sinful humanity! Wake up, I say, from your slumber. Stay awake and pray to be able to withstand these terrible times. I, My beloved, have exhausted all avenues of communication. Console My Mother, humanity. She tirelessly works on your behalf to appease My Father's anger. Many, My daughter, will cry bitterly over their sins when they wake up to the state of their souls. I too am crying over the sins of this pitiful humanity. Oh My sorrow! Who can fathom the sorrow of My heart. Oh please, My chosen ones consecrated to My heart, ATONE** (I feel it cannot be emphasized enough, the necessity to atone, to make reparation, and to persevere.). **Into a million pieces they have torn My heart, they have torn My heart to shreds. You who love Me can console Me. You who die for love of Me will experience the fulness of My love. Oh, daughter of My heart, weep, weep and more. Sorrow is coming to the earth as never before. I, JESUS, HAVE SPOKEN, IT SHALL BE DONE!"**

Here I am crying; here Jesus' voice is stern, commanding and firm as if He speaks with His Father's authority. Jesus is hurt beyond words and is angry. The effect of this message on me was heartbreaking and I was filled with the desire to make much more reparation to console Jesus.

When you read these words on paper they are nothing compared to how and in what way they were said. They were like someone speaking as though they are dying of a broken heart. Jesus' heart is crushed by our sins, our rejection of Him, our indifference to Him and to His and His Holy Mother's appeals. He is begging and pleading with us to amend our lives and make reparation for our sins.

*Two Biblical passages explain in detail the great chastisement to come. They are the entire 24th Chapter of Matthew, and

Luke 17:20-37. The Collegeville Biblical Commentary (The Liturgical Press, Collegeville, Minnesota, 1988), used with permission, follows:

THE COMING OF THE REIGN OF GOD:
Luke 17:20-37

"When Jesus sent the seventy-two disciples on their preaching mission at the beginning of His journey toward Jerusalem, He told them to proclaim the nearness of the reign of God (10:11). Earlier He had sent the Twelve to announce His reign (9:2). As he proceeds toward Jerusalem, the question arises, when will the reign of God come? Jesus answers first that the reign is already present (vv. 20-21) and then speaks of the definitive establishment of the kingdom at the end of the world (vv. 22-37).

The establishment of God's reign was expected with the coming of the Messiah (see 3:15). This would be the day of the Lord, a time of judgement and reward (Joel 2:1-2; 3:4-5). Jesus tells the Pharisees that knowledge of the time of the day of the Lord is not important. What is crucial is to recognize the presence of God's reign already in their midst. Jesus' ministry is the clear sign that God's reign has begun. No matter how clearly Jesus stated that the end cannot be calculated (v. 20; Mark: 13:32-33) and that its timing is not a question to be concerned with (Acts 1:6-8), the question continued to arise as He went toward Jerusalem (19:11) and afterward in the Church. Today it is still a major concern for many Christians, and their concern is still misplaced. Jesus' teaching on the question could not be clearer. Don't waste your time looking for signs and listening to clever calculations. Be aware that the reign of God is already in your midst; unless you give His present reign your full attention now, you will not be ready for the return of the Son of Man when it does occur. And no one can know when that will happen.

After calling attention to the present reality of God's reign, Jesus turns to His disciples to explain what is still to come. The presence of God's reign does not mean that the trials are over; there is still much suffering in store for Jesus (v. 25) and for His followers (v. 22). The disciples will be desperate for the Coming of the Son of Man, and this will lead them to follow false prophets and misleading theories about His appearance. But when it happens, the appearance of the Son of Man will not be subtle or

mysterious. Everyone will know. It will be as vivid as lightning across the sky. The contrast of the Son of Man's glory with suffering that must precede will make His Coming even more evident.

No matter when it happens, people will be unprepared. Worldly pursuits will captivate them, as they captivated those who lived in the days of Noah before the flood and the inhabitants of Sodom right up to the day of its destruction. That is why Jesus emphasizes the importance of recognizing the presence now of God's reign. It must govern our lives now, not just at the end; otherwise we will not be prepared to leave when the sudden call comes. One who is concerned about his possessions (14:33) will try to save them and be lost himself. Lot's wife is remembered as a person who was too attached to refrain from looking back (Gen 19-17, 26; see Luke 9:62).

The examples of the two men and the two women illustrate the suddenness of the coming of Christ and the readiness or unreadiness He will find. This has nothing to do with the "Rapture", a modern perversion of the scriptural teaching, which interprets these and the corresponding texts elsewhere (see Matt 24:37-41) as a description of the separation of good and evil people before the final Coming. Verse 36 is omitted in most versions because it is a scribal insertion taken from Matt 24:40, adding the example of the two men in the field to Luke's text. The proverb about the carcass and the vultures corresponds to the image of the lightning (v. 24). Jesus closes the instruction with a final stress on the dominant theme: the coming of the day of the Son of Man will be unmistakable. Meanwhile, do not devote your time and energy to signs and calculations, but to living in readiness."

1994

150.

Pray for My lost children

1 January 1994 *Saturday, Solemnity of Mary, Mother of God*

Holy Mother:

"My dear children, I wish to bless each and everyone here present on this, the beginning of a new year. Children so dear to My heart, God is very pleased with your sacrifices and efforts, for this the Holy Spirit will give you gifts in abundance. I, your Holy Mother, am with you all at every moment especially during your Cenacles (Prayer Groups). **I wish to tell you that I will be guiding everything. Do not worry when events around you seem alarming. It is necessary that these things happen. You are truly My little consecrated children so dear to My heart. I thank you for your consolation and your comfort which you have constantly given Me throughout the year, and Jesus, My Son, King of all kings, will reward each one of you in eternal Paradise. Behold your Mother, so sorrowful at the coming of a new year. Continue to pray with Me for God's mercy on the world and all My lost children. This I ask in Jesus' name. I bless you in the name of the Father and of the Son and of the Holy Spirit."**

151.

Through your pain and suffering many will be converted

6 January 1994 *Thursday* *Epiphany*

Holy Mother:

"Dear daughter, I do not wish you to be so troubled. This does not come from My Son. Try to trust more in the mercy of God. My daughter, I see you are in great need of assistance. I am beside you as I speak. Be not afraid, I will not abandon you. I do hear your prayers and I will help you

to continue. This short time is for the salvation of the world. Through your pain and suffering many are being converted. Offer it to Me and My Son and We will bless you and it will be to your greatest joy in Paradise. Protect yourself from the Evil One. He is very active in your life. Be strong in prayer. To combat him call on St. Michael for help. I wish you to pray the Novena to the Sacred Heart and Sr. Faustina to assist you in everything. Pray for patience, fortitude and the gift of discernment and also joy. Do not worry about your family and children. I will bless them and protect them with My mantle. God will also help you to be the person He wants you to be through the grace of the Holy Spirit. I bless you from My heart. Go in peace."

152.

Trust in Me, I will provide

6 January 1994 *Thursday 12.15 am* *Epiphany*

Jesus:

"My beloved daughter, it is I, Jesus. My daughter, do not be saddened and anxious, I am with you. It is My desire that you put your family's needs first before everything (i. e. before prayer groups and charity to others while of course giving God His due place). **I will provide the rest. Try to find a way, if you can, to do less work outside as you are needed more at home. It is not good for the children. I desire you to be there for them more as they need supervision and they need you. Your children do not benefit from you working outside."**

Geraldine: *"Lord, do You want me to give up work?"*

Jesus: **"Yes."**

Geraldine: *"Lord, I am frightened."*

Jesus: **"Daughter, trust in Me, I will provide, do not worry."**

Geraldine: *"Lord, do You not even want me to work one or two days only?"*

Jesus: **"My daughter, you are trying to do too much. Your home life is suffering."**

Geraldine: *"But Lord, what about my husband? He will not be happy."*

Jesus: **"My child, assure him, it is for the best."**

153.

Come adore and love your God

January 1994

Jesus:

"Daughter, come rest in My heart. Come, I long to be with you. Be in Me and I will be in you. Adore and love your God, who delights in souls that are close to Me. Come, I, Jesus, am waiting – love Me, adore Me, console Me, glorify Me. Give Me what I long for most (souls).

My Mother loves you, comfort Her also."

Geraldine: *"Goodnight, Lord."*

Jesus: **"Come."** He invites me to pray more; to meditate more on His passion.

154.

Rejoice, for I am coming soon to give you your reward

24 January 1994 *Monday* *St. Francis de Sales Memorial*

Jesus:

"Daughter, it is I, Jesus. Write this down for one and all. Children of My most Sacred Heart, I am with you in spirit. Comfort one another as I would comfort you. Love one another and forgive all offences. My Adversary is playing with each one of you (exploiting each one's weaknesses to the detriment of God's work)**, do not let him deceive you. Pray for forgiveness and discernment. Be on your guard always against the evil that surrounds you. Be last in everything,**

humble and meek as I am. Do no harm to anyone, keep your eyes on Me and if you must suffer, offer it to Me and My Mother and We will bless you for it and it will be to your greatest joy in Heaven. I have given you to each other as a gift to help and instruct one another. Do it with simplicity and love, seeking only to help and comfort. Do not judge anyone, lest you be judged yourself. I, the Eternal One, am with each one of you. Be in Me and I will be your strength. Suffer, to make up for the sins in the world and then rejoice for I, Jesus, am coming soon to give you your reward, which will be never-ending. I bless you in the name of the Father and of the Son and of the Holy Spirit."

155.

Consider the Religious life

27 January 1994 *Thursday* *St. Angela Merici*
Optional Memorial

Today I got a phone call from a young man, who asked if I would pray for him, and if I would ask Jesus if he could share in His passion for the salvation of souls. At first, I was surprised but I prayed for him.

Holy Mother:

"Tell My son .... that My Son, Jesus, is very pleased with his desire to suffer for souls in this way. However, it is not My Son's will that he suffer in this way. But it would be very pleasing to God if he will consider a vocation in the Religious life. For this he is being called and it will be to his greatest joy in Heaven. There are other ways he can suffer for souls by fasting, sacrifices, mortifications, etc." When I told him this message, he was extremely happy and told me he has been thinking of being a Priest for years and was overjoyed at this confirmation.

The next day he rang me and told me he was in a car accident. Their van hit a semi-trailer and flipped over, three people in the van were seriously injured and he was sitting in the front and

instead of the windscreen smashing inwards, it went outwards, and he was the only one not injured in the crash. He said at first he was frightened, then he was filled with hope and confidence as it seemed to him that God had called him to be a Priest and so he was not going to die. He said he approached a Parish Priest and he is trying to arrange for him to go into a monastery to train for theology and complete his studies in Year 11. I was so happy that through the encouragement of the message he was filled with enthusiasm to be a Priest.

"I praise and thank You, my Jesus and Holy Blessed Mother, I love You and adore You with every beat of my heart. Oh, Jesus, how can we ever repay your goodness. Dear Jesus, my Love, my Light and my Life, I adore You profoundly in the Blessed Sacrament. Dear Jesus, I beg for forgiveness for the sins I have committed throughout my life. Help me please, to always praise, honour, worship, love and adore You in everything I say and do. Oh, Sacrament Most Holy, oh Sacrament Divine, all Praise and all Thanksgiving be every moment Thine. Blessed be God forever!"

156.

Time is of the essence

28 January 1994 *Friday* *St. Thomas Aquinas Memorial*

Holy Mother:

"It is My desire that you share the intimacy that My Son, Jesus, has with you, with everyone, so that My children can see the greatness and goodness of God. *("But, Holy Mother, wouldn't I lose graces?")* **My child, time is of the essence. Souls will be lost if you do not tell them all about My Son. You will not lose graces by telling them – only if you do not do God's will. My Son wishes to share the same intimacy with all His children."**

157.

I wish you to appease My anger

1 February 1994 *Tuesday 12.00 pm*

Geraldine: *"Lord, how does it make You feel when people will not listen?"*

Jesus:

"My dear beloved, how would you feel if you gave your last drop of blood in agony for someone, and they said it is too depressing to think about it. I don't want to know. I wish you to appease My anger, I wish you to make reparation for souls such as this. Imagine, if you can, how I would feel. My agony is beyond imagination. Offer such souls to Me, pray for them, console your God and make up for those who wound Me, I will allow My Precious Blood to flow on sinners when you do this."

158.

I rejoice in these Cenacles

(Rosary Prayer Groups)

1 February 1994 *Tuesday*

Jesus:

"My beloved daughter, it is I, Jesus, do not worry or fear that you will lose My love, I have loved you since the world began in spite of your misery. It is this misery that attracts Me to you more. My beloved, I have a message for your group:"

God the Father speaks:

"My dear children, it is I, God the Father. I, My little ones, have come to tell you of My happiness and delight in such as you, if only all could love Me like this. I rejoice in these Cenacles, I am watching everything and I unite with you

whenever you worship and praise Me and My Son, and honour Mary. I implore you to listen well to My teaching and My word, put into practice what you hear and share your troubles with one another. I encourage this, for sharing is good and the Holy Spirit speaks to you through one another. My children, I am the Eternal Father, My Son is coming soon to judge the living and the dead*, do not let Him come and find you unprepared. Prepare now as you would for a feast, because I want you to rejoice, only prepare spiritually, for each will be given what he deserves. I bless you. Go in peace."

159.

Tell people about My love

1 February 1994 *Tuesday*

Holy Mother:

"Tell my son .... :

Thank you for your kindness and thoughtfulness. I love you very much and I rejoice in your decision to become a Priest, and Heaven rejoices. Dear son, your Guardian Angel saved your life in the car accident, praise and thank him and My Son, too. Continue, My son, to tell more people about Me and My love, I will bless you for this. Go in peace and do not be troubled."

* *"Judge the dead" seems definitely to refer to the Second Coming, the Final Judgement. Nevertheless "soon" is God's timing, not ours. See Revelations, chapter 22, verse 12. What is important is to be prepared. There is a definite urgency to prepare.*

160.

Divine Inspirations

4 February 1994 *First Friday 1.00 pm*

Holy Mother:

"I wish a book to be published entitled 'Divine Inspirations from Jesus and Mary' and picture of Our Two Hearts on the front encircled, I wish the writing in front to be in gold and the book to be the colour red in honour of My Son's Sacred Heart. On the back a picture of the Divine Mercy to remind My children of My Son's mercy. Do not worry about this event, I will provide, pray that God's will be done. The task ahead of you is great but I will provide everything. Tell .... to pray and act as soon as possible. I bless you in the name of the Father and of the Son and of the Holy Spirit."

161.

My house is empty

12 February 1994 *Saturday 10.00 am*

Holy Mother:

"My dear child, I have called you here to console Me and My Son. Here you go to Confession (Reconciliation) **and to Mass and receive Holy Communion often. My child, see how My Son's house is empty** (a new church often closed and empty), **come often and comfort Him. I greatly desire this. My child, I wish you to pray for more vocations. Do not worry about the future, it is in God's hands, be always at peace."**

162.

We must all pray for what we need

14 February 1994 *Monday* *Sts. Cyril and Methodius Memorial*

Geraldine: *"Oh Mother, some people are disappointed they don't get answers to problems straight away."*

Holy Mother:

"My child, be at peace. My child, many people will want quick, fast answers to their problems. But, My child, through you I wish My children to come closer to My Son through prayer. We must all pray for what we need. God desires it to be so. So do not worry about anything and be at peace."

163.

Pray for the success of this Mission

14 February 1994 *Monday* *Sts. Cyril and Methodius Memorial*

Geraldine: *"Dear Mother, what should I do about all the messages lost?"*

Holy Mother:

"My child, I will give them to you again. Do not worry. Pray for the success of this mission. Pray and do not be concerned about anything."

164.

Your human nature is frail and weak

14 February 1994 Monday *Sts. Cyril and Methodius Memorial*

Geraldine: *"Mother, why do I doubt?"*

Holy Mother:

"Daughter, your human nature is frail and weak. Only constant contact with Me will sustain you. I, My child, love you. Don't worry, I will help you carry your cross. I understand your concerns. You do not offend Me. I am here to help you to do My Son's will. We will provide everything, be at peace and don't worry. Set aside one hour per day to write and I will give you the lost messages."

Geraldine: *"Holy Mother, I feel so bad, because I doubt."*

Holy Mother: **"Child, I am your Mother and with God anything is possible, trust in Me."**

Geraldine: *"Mother, I am worried about the work on the home extensions."*

Holy Mother: **"Daughter, pray to Jesus about this. Leave it in His hands. Pray for now and be at peace."**

165.

In you God is glorified

14 February 1994 *Monday Sts. Cyril and Methodius Memorial*

Geraldine: *"Holy Mother, why did God pick such a useless instrument (as me)?"*

Holy Mother:

"To show, My child, that this work could not possibly come from you. In this way He is glorified. The important thing for you to do is to pray and write. This is all My Son requires of you; and fast for this intention."

166.

Leave everything in My Son's hands

14 February 1994 Monday, Sts. Cyril and Methodius Memorial

Holy Mother:

"Tell .... that I wish her to say a Novena to the Sacred Heart and My Son will answer her prayer in due time. My child (i. e. Geraldine), **be at peace and leave it all in My Son's hands and soon He will answer your prayer. I love you, My daughter, go in peace."**

167.

I speak to your conscience

14 February 1994 Monday Sts. Cyril and Methodius Memorial

A Guardian Angel:

"I have been given the care of .... I am guiding and enlightening him in everything. My work is to bring him as close as possible to Jesus, my Master. I help him in many ways. I speak to his conscience and I prevent him from falling into the Evil One's traps. This soul is rich in good works and I am very happy to be his constant companion in life. His soul is very beautiful. Tell him to talk to me more and that I so much desire a closer relationship with him."

168.

Receive the Sacraments daily

14 February 1994 Monday *Sts. Cyril and Methodius Memorial*

Geraldine: *"Do You have a message?"*

Holy Mother:

"Oh, yes, My child, write for souls. Dear children, your Holy Mother speaks to you. Children so dear to My heart, help Me please, I beg you. Quickly, I tell you, I suffer so much. Tell everyone you can that the Lord is coming. Oh, My children, My sorrow is immense, I see so much catastrophe ahead of you, come quickly to Me, all of you, for protection. Pray, pray, pray as never before. Help and console one another. I love you all and want you close to Me to save you from the Evil One, who hates you and wants to destroy you and your families. Receive the Sacraments daily. Time is of the essence. My Son's wrath is about to come upon the whole world. Pray, pray and offer all in reparation. Pray more, love more, suffer more. Walk with your Mother the road to Calvary, along with My Divine Son Jesus. My children, God has sent Me to warn you, listen to the voice of the prophets,* as you cannot imagine what the Father has prepared for those who offend Him continually. Pray, I beg you, for My lost children. (Here Our Lady is crying and is so pitiful I feel so sorry for Her as Her heart is breaking.)

My beloved children who are faithful to Me, console your sorrowful Mother in constant prayer, penance, reparation and fasting. I bless you in the name of the Father, and of the Son and of the Holy Spirit."

---

* *Those who genuinely bear God's message for the world today.*

169.

Pray a great deal for unbelievers

18 February 1994 *Lenten Friday*

Holy Mother:

To ....

"Tell My son, My heart is aching for My lost children, pray a great deal for unbelievers, in doing so you are praying for your future."

170.

Trust Me

18 February 1994 *12.15 pm* *Lenten Friday*

Jesus:

"My dear daughter, it is I, Jesus, I wish to speak to ...., write this down: 'My beloved one, why do you doubt Me? Don't you know I love you and I live in you? Don't you know I desire you more than you desire Me? I will never let you go, My heart is an abyss of love for you. Do not worry when I withdraw, I do so only to bring you closer to Me; as silver and gold are tested I too test those I love. Be at peace and rejoice in My love, allow Me to penetrate you with My goodness, rest in Me and My love will transform you. I, your God, long for you to trust Me, by this you will love Me more. Be at peace for I am coming soon to give you your reward. I love you.' "

171.

Behold My heart

11 March 1994 *12.00 pm* *Lenten Friday*

Holy Mother:

"My beloved daughter, write down what I say, I want all humanity to hear My messages.

Tell My children (i. e. those devoted to Our Lady), **My heart yearns for their conversion, and for the conversion of all My children. I wish you, dear chosen one, to pray for those furthest from My heart, I love you all and I am helping each one of you. Behold My heart, My daughter, which at this moment is so wounded, console your sorrowful Mother who weeps at so much sin. Help Me please, I beg you. Pray more with Me for the sinful world so steeped in immorality. Unite your suffering to Mine, and Jesus, My Divine Son, will bless you for it. My daughter, the world is now approaching its terrifying purification. Pray very much, let your whole life be a prayer. Do not worry about little things, when you pray, God will make all things possible. I beg you, My children, support Me now in My greatest need. My children, I want to tell you of the devastation which lies ahead, weep and pray for the sins in the world, God is greatly offended and is about to punish. Listen to Me, My beloved children so dear to My heart, I am preparing you now before this happens, stay close to Me even in the greatest trials because you will be put to the test; call on My Son and Me to sustain you always. My child, I do not wish to alarm you but only to bring you closer to My heart, in preparation for the greatest chastisement since the world began – which is to come. Pray, pray, pray."**

172.

Do not give up the struggle

11 March 1994 *9.00 pm* *Lenten Friday*

Holy Mother:

"My dear children, I love you and I bless each one of you. My beloved children, I wish you all to continue to persevere in prayer with Me and My Divine Son. If you, My children, give up, who will console My Son? Who will appease His anger? Who will make reparation? The reward is great. I am, I assure you, close to each one of you, do not give up the struggle. I know your troubles and temptations, but, My children, continue towards your goal, towards your

crown of glory. The Heavenly Father is greatly pleased with your efforts and will bless you abundantly, the Angels and Saints await you to pray, speak to them. I, My children, have been greatly consoled by your prayers and please continue to console Me in this My hour of need and in Paradise, My children, I will be waiting to greet each one of you. I am tireless in My petitions before God for you, such is My love for you. Be not afraid of the events happening around you or in the future, you are a chosen generation, My Father hand-picked you for this, the Triumph of My Immaculate Heart, be of good cheer and courage, I am with you always.

Be on your guard against My Adversary who hates you on account of the souls you snatch from him, stay in My heart and I will protect you always. The Coming of My Son is very near, stay awake and pray. I will help you and your Guardian Angels will guide and protect you. I love you and I bless each one of you. Go in peace."

173.

I give you My Motherly blessing

12 March 1994 *Lenten Saturday*

Holy Mother:

To ....

"My dear son, I love you, be at peace and ask the Holy Spirit for the gifts you require. He will let know if this (something he was proposing to do) **is right for you at this time. I give you My Motherly blessing."**

174.

The Rosary is the weapon

15 March 1994 *Lenten Tuesday*

In front of the Blessed Sacrament (after Holy Communion)

We came to pray the Rosary and Divine Mercy Prayers. When we started, Our Lady appeared on the right side of the Tabernacle, as I was praying before the Blessed Sacrament. She was all in white with gold sandals and a crown on Her head. She was looking at us with great love and joy, so happy to see us there. First, She said, **"Tell .... not to be discouraged, I will help her to pray."** Then She touched another person's head (who was suffering terribly at that time) in a loving Motherly gesture. She was so happy to see us. Then She held up the Rosary in both hands and said, **"Don't forget, the Rosary is the weapon."** Then I said, *"Holy Mother, where is Jesus?"** And She replied, **"He is in your hearts."** Then She said, **"I bless you and God blesses you all."**

175.

Offer more sacrifices

18 March 1994 *6.30 pm* *Lenten Friday*

Holy Mother:

"My child, tell My son I wish him to help you to come closer to Me. In all things be united to God. Ask Father to help you to pray more for the success of this mission. Go in peace. Offer more sacrifices to Me and My Son."

---

* *We were in front of the Blessed Sacrament and I thought I'd see Jesus (not Our Lady). Spiritual Director's comment: Although Jesus is truly present in the Blessed Sacrament it seems that here His presence in the hearts of the faithful is emphasized.*

176.

Pray and be at peace

18 March 1994 *Lenten Friday*

Father was very concerned for a Religious.

Holy Mother:

"Say seven Our Fathers, seven Hail Marys and seven Glory Be's". This was after I had said prayers from a prayer book. She still wanted more prayers before She would speak. *"Holy Mother, have I done the right thing* (after saying more prayers)*?"* I think She wanted me to pray more for this Religious before She would give a message.

Our Lady said: **"Yes, My child, write down what I say. Tell Father not to be distressed, the situation is not as bad as it appears. I will intercede on his behalf. Tell him to say the Novena to the Sacred Heart for God's guidance in this matter and not to worry, I will help and provide. My son, be at peace. I am with you. Pray and do not alarm yourself any more but trust in God's mercy. I love you and bless you both."** This message proved to be true as the situation was found to be less serious than at first imagined.

177.

Do not be afraid, I am preparing everything

21 March 1994 *Lenten Monday*

Jesus:

"My child, tell My son .... to do that which is within his power to help My messages to be spread far and wide for many souls can be saved through them. I wish My children to help Me to prepare humanity for My Coming, go tell everyone to prepare for I am coming as a just judge to one and all. Daughter, do not be afraid, I am preparing all, trust Me and pray."

178.

Persevere, beloved ones

21 March 1994 *Lenten Monday*

Jesus:

"My child, it is I, Jesus. My beloved of My heart, I have come to console you and My loved ones in all your difficulties. Children, do not be afraid, I am with you, I assure you I will not let you be tested beyond that of which you are capable. I wish you to suffer with Me to ease My pains and appease My anger. Think, My beloved children, of the joy that awaits you in Paradise and all its splendour for all eternity. I will raise you up as My sign to all of that which God wants from His children, faithfulness and love. Hold on, My beloved ones, for I, Jesus, am coming soon to give you your reward for persevering in My love. I love you and I bless you. Go in peace."

179.

I will help you

24 March 1994 *Lenten Thursday*

Holy Mother:

For ....

"Tell My son, in all his work I am with him, and I rejoice in all his work done for the salvation of souls. Tell My son, I wish him to continue this work which I have entrusted to him and the grace of God will sustain him in everything. Tell him to persevere to the end in all I ask and to be faithful to all that to which God is calling him. My son, you are very dear to My heart. I love you beyond that which you can imagine, do not fear anything or anyone. I will help in all your needs. ...., know that My Son Jesus rejoices in you, and know the Angels and Saints are eager to intercede so that more graces may come to you. Be strong and courageous in the face of adversity, I especially will be your light in the darkness. My son, I love you and I bless you, go in peace."

180.

I am by your side

27 March 1994 *Palm Sunday*

Holy Mother:

"Dear daughter, your suffering is from the Most High (i. e. God permits this suffering for a spiritual good). **Accept and offer all with joy. I will sustain you, do not fear, I am by your side. Do not distress yourself. I understand your weakness. Jesus, My Son, is bringing you closer to His heart through this suffering. Offer it and be at peace, I will do the rest. Family members will respond to more love, show them more affection and they will respond more, show them how to love more. I love you and bless you and this family."**

181.

Implore My Mercy for sinners

28 March 1994 *Monday* *Holy Week*

Jesus:

"My children, faithful followers of My Mother, I give you My special blessing in this Holy Week."

God the Father and Jesus (They seemed to be One: That is, Jesus seems to speak with all the weight of His Father's authority behind Him):

"Children, listen, your Father speaks. I wish you to make amends for the indifference shown to Me in the Blessed Sacrament, prepare more before (i. e. for Mass, to make up for those who do not). **Fast, especially now in the time of My passion, do not worry, I will help you. Implore My mercy for sinners, make up for all I am suffering and appease My anger. I bless you and the Holy Trinity blesses you, be at peace."**

182.

My sorrow is immense

1 April 1994 *Good Friday*

Holy Mother (during the prayers at a Prayer Group):

"My beloved daughter so dear to My heart, write down what I say.

Dear children, I am happy to see you come in such great numbers, My heart is joyful because of this. As you know, today My sorrow and My Son's are immense, make reparation often to console My dearly beloved Son, who each day is crucified. I am, My children, among you today as I was with the Apostles in the upper room when the Holy Spirit descended upon them. I give you My Motherly Blessing and I assure you I am close to each one of you on this sorrowful day.The grace of God will sustain you in every trial, so love one another as My Jesus loves you, and be at peace."

183.

I give you My heart

1 April 1994 *Good Friday*

Holy Mother:

"My child, I have a special message for My son, ... Tell him I love him and I am rejoicing in him.

My beloved son, I am guiding everything, do not be concerned, I am with you always guiding, helping and consoling you. My son so dear to My heart, I give you My heart today as I rejoice in your goodness and love for Me and My Divine Son. Be mindful of My presence beside you in every difficulty. I am, My son, happy to rest in your love. Go in peace."

184.

Good Friday

1 April 1994

Today, during our Prayer Group, as I prayed the Sorrowful Mysteries, Jesus suddenly appeared to me on the Cross in agony. The sight was more than I could bear. I felt my heart was going to break with grief. I was sobbing within myself and I had to beg Our Holy Mother to help me take control of myself. Jesus then said, **"Behold My Wounds!"** At this moment I felt completely broken in every way physically, emotionally and mentally. It was like being crushed, overwhelmed and being unable to do anything about it, being totally helpless. I don't know whether this was what Jesus was feeling but it could have been. The look in Jesus' eyes when He spoke was one of great love and compassion. It was like the look of a married person at a beloved spouse where the couple are united in love: One turns to the other and says, "Beloved, will you accept suffering for love of me and will you help me?" The plea is as from a dying heart and is made out of the greatest love for the one to whom it is addressed. The appeal in Jesus' eyes to help Him was heart-rending. There are no words strong enough to properly describe this and one wanted to do all one could to respond. Jesus here reveals how His heart is wounded and how compassionate it is towards us. If we knew of the suffering of His heart we would console Him much more by amending our lives. But Jesus respects our free will and He leaves us completely free in our response. It is love alone that draws us to do His will and not any kind of emotional coercion. Satan would do anything he could to prevent people from knowing Jesus as He reveals Himself here. This scene passed, and then I saw Our Holy Mother sobbing at the foot of the Cross, with Jesus in Her arms. I thought I was going to die of sorrow. Only with supernatural help could I bear it.

Geraldine: *"Jesus, grant that I may serve no one except You, that I may know You, love You and live by Your help, for You and with You now and forever. Amen."*

185.

Easter Sunday

3 April 1994

I was watching the "Ben-Hur" film, not thinking of anything at all, when the Sacred Heart picture in front of me glowed with a light. I thought the ceiling light might be shining on it. Then I heard, **"I am resurrected, praise and thank My Father, and pray the Rosary in thanksgiving."** I had the baby asleep in my arms, so I put him down to go and look at the clock, and it was 12.10 am, Easter Sunday morning. I was completely taken by surprise, and prayed three Rosaries.

186.

Go to the Bishop

4 April 1994 *Easter Monday*

Holy Mother:

"Tell my son Fr. ...., it is My desire he along with you go to Bishop .... soon. Tell him all I am asking of you. Prepare for this meeting with much prayer, and I will bless you and be by your side."

187.

Saint Gertrude

5 April 1994 *Easter Tuesday*

Today, I spoke with St. Gertrude. She said, **"Beloved of My Divine Master, I have come to tell you that Our Beloved Master has desired that you say Novenas to the Saints for .... so his heart may be touched, and for the success of this mission. I have come to help you to prepare for future trials. This mission has been sent to you by God to bring souls closer to His heart and to prepare for His Coming. Be not**

afraid of anything. God is with you. I will assist you often. Pray more for holy Priests."

188.

My heart rejoices in this mission

7 April 1994 *Easter Thursday*

Holy Mother:

"My dear child, I want you to write down what I say so you can reflect on it later. My dear daughter, know that I love you, My heart rejoices in this mission. Give praise, thanks and glory to God for His great goodness. Be sincere in all that you do for love of God."

At a Conference 9/10th April, 1994:

189.

I am so happy

9 April 1994 *Saturday after Easter*

During the Conference, I see an interior vision of Heaven rejoicing in our honouring of Mary, Our Mother. I am so happy.

190.

I will open the floodgates of My love

9 April 1994 *Saturday after Easter*

Jesus:

"This weekend, I will open the floodgates of My love upon you. An abundance of graces will be given to those present."

191.

Give these children of Mine encouragement

10 April 1994 *Second Sunday of Easter*

At the Conference

Holy Mother:

"Go to these people, they will help spread My messages. I want you to tell them, I love and rejoice in their mission and I bless their undertakings. Go in peace. Go to them after Mass, as before Mass you must prepare for My Son (whom you will receive in Holy Communion). Tell them of My Son's love.

My child, how I rejoice in this, My heart is greatly consoled and Jesus, My Divine Son, has given Me permission to take each one of you into My Immaculate Heart, and to give you My love, peace and joy. I love and give each one of you My special Motherly Blessing (i. e. all singers, organizers, speakers, participants, etc.). **Give these children of Mine encouragement. Praise and thank them for what they were doing for God."** (Having done so I was amazed at how much they needed this and how they appreciated it, even the international singers were very grateful for this encouragement.)

After Adoration and Benediction

Jesus: **"Behold your God! Daughter, love Me, behold Me. I rejoice in you, daughter, I am with you, you will not be deceived. Daughter, are you happy?"**

Geraldine: *"Yes, Lord."*

Jesus: **"Thank you, My child, go in peace."**

192.

If only all could love Me as you do!

11 April 1994 *Monday* *St. Stanislaus Optional Memorial*

Today, I am in the most dreadful pain. Nothing will ease it. I am nauseous and have a severe pain in my head etc., and I can't speak or move. At one point, I cry out to Jesus to help me in my anguish. I say, *"Lord, I am an abyss of misery, less than the dirt beneath Your feet. I am not worthy to even speak to You. But in spite of my wretchedness and sinfulness, I come before You relying only on Your Divine Mercy."* (Here I realize, that without it, I could not come before Him and I ask Him to help me.) To my amazement He speaks to me with the greatest amount of love and affection. I am amazed at His goodness. I feel His unconditional love and that I am the greatest sinner alive and He stoops down so low and speaks to me as though He loves me immensely despite my sins.

Jesus:

"Beloved of My heart, I take delight in dwelling in your soul. If only all could love Me as you do; My Sacred Heart rejoices in such souls. Be not afraid, for I, your Lord and Master, am with you." (When Jesus fills my heart with so much love and peace, I feel I am not here, but in Heaven, and it gives me all I need to endure anything. Praise be Jesus and Mary.)

193.

Wake up, humanity, and console your God

12 April 1994 *Tuesday 3.00 pm*

Jesus (He was speaking with anger and firmness in His voice):

"I am hurt greatly by the sins of humanity. I will not let those who offend Me go unpunished. I have warned people many times of My Coming, now I am about to strike, woe to this wicked generation who with its corruption and perversity have greatly offended Heaven. I, the Lord God,

will not have mercy on them when My judgement comes. Wake up, humanity, and console your God! The blood of the martyrs cries out in vengeance. Wake up, I say, from the sleep of death, for the world is about to be rocked to its very foundations. Cry out to the Father now to appease God's anger. Be happy to suffer for My sake, only through you (the good people who make reparation) **shall My anger be appeased** (again I felt His great anger). **Go in peace."**

Jesus: **"Tell Father of your suffering."**

Geraldine: "But Jesus, why?"

Jesus: **"So he can pray that you receive the courage and strength to do My will."**

"Daughter, let it be known, your God is being crucified daily* **and I wish My chosen ones to make up for all I am suffering, tell them to continue to appease My anger. Tell the Priests to pray more. That is all for now, I do not wish to speak on this subject any more. I love you, My child, suffer with Me for souls."**

194.

I feel the delights and splendour of Heaven

13 April 1994 | *Wednesday* | *St. Martin I, Pope Optional Memorial*

Jesus:

Today again I suffer in pain and Jesus assures me it (the suffering) is from Him to appease His anger, and for souls. He shows me how tiny our suffering is here, compared to all eternity, which is never-ending. Our life is like a dot in eternity. Here I feel the delights and splendour, the love and peace that those, who are in Jesus' presence, possess. It is like experiencing

---

* *Jesus is gloriously enthroned in Heaven, and His risen body cannot suffer anymore. How then is He "crucified daily"?* **1.** *Sins (including those committed today) were the cause of Jesus' crucifixion.* **2.** *Jesus is crucified daily in His mystical body, "Whatever you do to the least of My brothers, you do to Me."*

a slice of Heaven. I can suffer anything in this state.* *"My Lord, my Light and my Life, I adore Thee profoundly. You are my everything, I wish to praise and adore You continuously, now and forever, for Your goodness."*

195.

Pray for My suffering children

16 April 1994 *Saturday*

Holy Mother (as She is speaking I have in mind victims of wars, those in concentration camps, those at the mercy of terrorists):

"My child, I wish to tell My children of the sorrow in My heart. My children, pray for the persecuted, for the suffering children and adults who are in great danger as we speak. Pray, fast and help in any way, this is My Motherly wish that you console them and Me in this way. I will bless you and My Son will bless you abundantly for all your work on behalf of My suffering children. Gather My children together and ask them to hold vigils of prayer for this suffering humanity. I bless you and thank each one of you. Go in peace."

196.

Be at peace and pray

16 April 1994 *Saturday*

Holy Mother:

"My child, I wish all that My Son and I have spoken be written in the book. In this way My children will learn from the experiences and the teachings which We have given you over the years. Do not worry or be concerned about its distribution, God is guiding the entire mission. Let the Priests know what I have said and they will best discern everything. Be at peace and pray for this mission."

---

* *Jesus wants us to think of Heaven when we are suffering, because with our reward in view, we cope better.*

197.

Pray for this suffering humanity

23 April 1994 *Saturday* *St. George Optional Memorial*

Jesus:

In bed Saturday morning, a light descends upon me quite unexpectedly.

"Daughter, I wish you to pray often the chaplets of the Divine Mercy and the Holy Wounds and the fifteen decades of the Rosary for this terrible suffering humanity to appease My anger. All sins are offensive to Me.

Call on My Mother and She will help you to perfect yourself."*

198.

In silence and hiddenness

24 April 1994 *Sunday 1.00 pm* *Fourth Sunday of Easter*

Holy Mother:

"My child, I have a message for your group. My child, are you ready to write down what I say?"

Geraldine: *"Yes, Holy Mother, I am."*

Holy Mother: **"My child, I want Father, yourself and the leaders of the prayer groups to discuss future events. I have come to teach you how to pray. Your husbands will not be happy when you run yourselves down** (i. e. trying to do too many things outside the home)**. I wish you to be very involved in your family life and to be the heart of your home. Stay in your homes more and you will discover better ways of pleasing God and you will find more time for silence and prayer. I do not mind you joining together once or twice a week as long as it does not interfere with your daily duty. I, My children, am helping you to be holy mothers at home, not**

* *Jesus was firm and angry and I felt hardness or sternness because of the sins of the world.*

outside. Arrange a suitable time among yourselves for prayer gatherings that will benefit you all and suit everyone. Continue to receive Holy Communion daily and Confession often. Listen, My children, to the call of your Mother's heart: Pray more in the silence of your home, this is how you will work out your sanctification in silence and hiddenness. I bless each one of you, go in peace."

199.

Jesus is consoled

24 April 1994 *Fourth Sunday of Easter*

Holy Mother:

"Daughter, I have come to tell you how happy I am that you have done what My Son asked. Daughter, let it be known that Jesus is consoled. Happy are you who work for My Son, in you My Son will find great peace." (Here I see Our Lady, quite suddenly and unexpectedly. She comes full of joy and great delight, because the prayers have appeased Jesus' anger and consoled Him.)

200.

I rejoice in this

26 April 1994 *Tuesday 3.45 pm*

Geraldine: *"Holy Mother, did I do the right thing joining the Third Order (of a Religious Order)?"*

Holy Mother:

"My child, I am very happy you have chosen to consecrate your life more fully to My Son. These daughters (nuns) **are especially close to My Son, as they adore Him continuously. They will help you greatly in your spiritual life and you also may be of some help to them. I rejoice in this decision. Check with Father before you take the next step.**

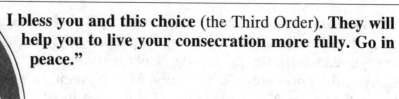

I bless you and this choice (the Third Order)**. They will help you to live your consecration more fully. Go in peace."**

201.

Pray to the Sacred Heart

29 April 1994 *Friday* *St. Catherine of Siena Memorial*

Dear Diary:

For some time now I have had to endure much suffering. I feel alone. If I hear Jesus speak, it seems at a distance. I am plagued with doubts and bad thoughts and I wish to be alone so I will not sin and wish to pray more in silence. My concentration seems to be gone, I feel like I am in a pit and cannot get out. I go to Confession and the Priest tells me he sees no sins, even though I feel I am full of sin and a wretch. Then, when I come out of Confession, I feel worse. I still feel a sinner and get no relief. I try to pray the Rosary and go to Mass, but I end up crying inconsolably. The next day I feel worse, like God has abandoned me, and my suffering is terrible. I didn't even feel like going to Mass, but I did not wish to offend Jesus. After Mass, I go before the Blessed Sacrament and pour out my heart to Jesus, offering my suffering to Him for the conversion of sinners. This is what He said:

Jesus:

"Protect yourself from the Evil One. He is very active in your life. Be strong in prayer. To combat him, call on St. Michael to help. I wish you to pray the Novena to the Sacred Heart and Sr. Faustina to assist you in everything. Pray for patience, fortitude and the gift of discernment and also joy. Do not worry about your family and children, I will bless them and protect them and keep them in My care. God the Father will also help you to be the person He wants you to be through the grace of the Holy Spirit. I bless you from My heart. Go in peace."

202.

I am preparing everything

29 April 1994 *Friday, St. Catherine of Siena Memorial*

Holy Mother:

"My child, do not worry, you are not displeasing Me by praying and asking favours for others. Daughter, always check with Father before you do anything. This is most pleasing to God.

Daughter, write down what I say. This is for the family of the little girl. Do not be sad or discouraged. I am preparing everything. Pray to your Father in Heaven for all your needs and do not distress yourself any further. I will sustain you when you have recourse to Me. Through her illness, the whole family will come closer to God and to Me. I bless you in the name of the Father, and of the Son and of the Holy Spirit."

203.

Pray always for whatever you need

29 April 1994 *Friday 10.00 pm* *St. Catherine of Siena Memorial*

Holy Mother:

"My dear child, it is I, Holy Mother, do not be afraid, for I will help you to overcome your weaknesses which My Adversary uses to keep you from reaching greater heights in the spiritual life. Pray the Novena to Sr. Faustina and My Son's Sacred Heart. Here you will draw supernatural strength abundantly. Pray always for whatever you need. Daughter, I see the desire of your heart. Don't distress yourself any further. God is with you. Rest in His Love and wait for Him to act. I love you, I thank you and I embrace you to My Motherly Heart. Be at peace."

204.

This humanity causes Me great suffering

30 April 1994 *Saturday* *St. Pius V, Pope*
Optional Memorial

After Mass, before the Blessed Sacrament

Jesus:

"Daughter, because of the goodwill in your heart and your love for Me, I am bestowing upon you many graces from My heart. I ask for your suffering because you help Me and it lessens My suffering when we share it. This humanity causes Me great suffering, so if I give you more, welcome it and I will delight your spirit and lift it to new heights. Oh, how My heart delights in souls such as yours. Beloved of My heart, adore Me, love Me, make up for all I am suffering. Make up for all the insults heaped upon Me. Adore your God. Worship Him with all your heart, soul, mind and body. I am eternal, I am infinite. Behold your God who loves you like no other. Rejoice in Me who am all Mercy. Daughter, the graces I give you will help you to overcome yourself and rise to new heights, together we will suffer for souls. Glorify Me, adore Me with roses of My Mother's Holy Rosary. Walk with Me to Calvary, wiping My brow as I walk. Caress My Wounds, make up for all I am suffering. Show Me very much love by helping Me to carry My cross, which at times is so heavy. Desire to uphold Me always and My heart will set your heart on fire with flames of My Divine Love. Rejoice in the gifts I give you and be always thankful to the Father, to My Mother and Myself who love you greatly. Enough for now. Rest in My love." After this I am changed from being depressed to feeling very happy. Jesus also said, **"Do not doubt. Behold your God who loves you with an everlasting love."**

205.

Prepare everything

3 May 1994 *Tuesday 12.15 pm* *Feast of Sts. Philip and James, Apostles*

Geraldine: *"Father has asked me to ask You what do we do next? Holy Mother, how do I know this is from You?"*

Holy Mother:

"Father will discern, continue to write, My child. I wish these messages to be shown to Bishop .... as soon as possible. I will bless this work, do not worry, only pray for the success of this mission, I will provide. Continue as Father said and prepare everything, write from each book all My Son has said (i. e. prepare for publication the messages originally written in several notebooks). **Again I tell you, this mission is entirely My Son's. Pray and work for its fulfilment. I bless you and your work. Be at peace. I love you."**

206.

I desire that you go to the Bishop

3 May 1994 *Tuesday* *Feast of Sts. Philip and James, Apostles*

Holy Mother:

"My child, you tell Father .... of My desire that you go to Bishop ...."

207.

They are crucifying Me

6 May 1994 First Friday

At Adoration in front of the Blessed Sacrament

Jesus:

"Dearly beloved of My heart, contemplate Me, behold your God, make up for all I am suffering. Daughter, I wish you to tell humanity of My great suffering, they have opened My Wounds and My Blood pours profusely."

I ask Him, *"Lord, how can I ease Your pain?"*

"Your prayers will heal My Wounds. Take Me off the Cross by your prayers and hold Me in your arms as My Mother did to Me, console your God. They are crucifying Me. I wish you to be united with Me each day. When you do not do so you wound Me, remember this when you are tempted. I have chosen you to be a prophet of this time. They will ridicule you for love of Me, persecute you and crucify you. But I will give you My Strength, Courage and Love. As My Father gave Me, so I will give you. The grace of God will sustain you."

After a while I noticed my legs were very stiff and painful and throbbing. I said, *"Lord, do I sit or kneel?"*

He said, **"If you could see Me, what would you do?"**

I said, *"I would be in AWE."*

And He answered, **"So be it!"**

Then He asked me to contemplate Him on the Cross in the mysteries of His Passion. I don't like to (as I find it distressing) but as I did as He wished, everything around me started to fade away and I was feeling no pain or stiffness. I was not aware of my body, I was with Jesus on the Cross and I felt all His suffering and anguish in my heart and I cried.* I felt so much love for Him then, that there would have been nothing I would not have done for Him. Then I saw His Mother weeping and He said, **"Behold My Mother, whose tears and suffering fall on deaf ears, console Her in Her grief."** He was more concerned about Her than Himself and His own pain. I felt His love for Her. He loves

* *I cry when I meditate on His Passion, as it upsets me.*

Her greatly and delights when we comfort Her. I see all this in front of me as if I was there, not here. Then I came back to reality and felt the pain and stiffness back again.

Then He said, **"Do what .... advised, spend one hour a day with Me. I need this time with you to converse with you, pray the fifteen decades daily.**

In the next ten weeks, I wish to prepare you to become an Oblate of the Third Order of .... (a Religious Order). **In your heart you will be more united to Me and better able to please Me. My child, remember, embrace Me and My cross, I bless you, be at peace."**

208.

I rejoice in your adoration of Me

7 May 1994 *First Saturday*

Jesus:

"My daughter, it is I, the Eternal One. I rejoice in your adoration last night. This is very pleasing to Me, continue to appease My anger in this way, and continue to encourage others to do the same."

209.

Pray and fast

8 May 1994 *Sixth Sunday of Easter*

Holy Mother:

"Daughter, I have a message for .... (I pray more and bless myself, because I hear Satan trying to stop this message).

Dear child, continue and be at peace, he cannot harm you. Tell My son, thank you for your prayers and sacrifices, I am answering your prayer. Beloved son, I am asking you to gather My children together to unite and to publish this book, 'Divine Inspirations', as soon as you can. My Son is not happy with the constant delays. Pray, fast, and act quickly, time is

so short and many souls are in despair and need to be fed. Feed My children, they are crying out to Me and I am choosing certain instruments to do this work. Be on the alert, the Evil One is waiting to devour all who partake in this, My work. Act quickly, having recourse to Me in your necessities. My son, help Me to quickly feed My children, who daily cry out to Me for justice. Hurry, My son, and quickly arrange everything. I am with you guiding you, listen to Me and be at peace. I love you very much."**

210.

Behold My Mother who loves you

12 May 1994 *Thursday* *Ascension of the Lord Solemnity*

Jesus:

"Beloved, go to your child, he comes first. Beloved, be at peace in spite of your suffering. Behold My Mother who loves you. Go in peace."

211.

Do not worry

12 May 1994 *Thursday* *Ascension of the Lord Solemnity*

Holy Mother:

For ....

"My child, what is spoken of is not of God. I wish the prayer of exorcism* to be said to obtain God's protection for the group. I will assist them in all their necessities. Be persevering in all goodness and My Son will bless you abundantly. Do not worry, the grace of God is with you

* *Disturbing things were happening at a prayer group, so I prayed about it. Of course – only the Bishop's representative can formally exorcise. Here the reference is to a simple prayer from a prayer book.*

always. Go in peace, My beloved children, for you have found great favour with My Son."

212.

Remember what is awaiting you

12 May 1994 *Thursday 2.30 pm* *Ascension of the Lord Solemnity*

Holy Mother:

"Tell My child .... I am with her and by her side in everything. Jesus, My Son, will help you cope better, do not despair, trust in God, He will sustain you. Pray and offer all to MY SON WHO IS THE LIGHT OF THIS WORLD* which is walking in darkness. Be of good cheer and courage and remember what is awaiting you, your eternal abode, Paradise in all its glory. Persevere in all your troubles and pray to the Saints to guide and help you, and your Guardian Angel will help you greatly. Speak to him often. I give My special Motherly Blessing to you and all your family. Go in peace."

213.

Be more united to Our Two Hearts

12 May 1994 *Thursday* *Ascension of the Lord Solemnity*

Holy Mother:

"Daughter of My heart, listen, I, your Mother, speak. Child, you feel My sorrow and My love. I give you this gift to enlighten you and to help you to continue to help others. Child, I love you immensely and I rely on you to help Me to fulfil My desires. I am closer to you now and am at present beside you."

* *Message of 14 June 1994 speaks of a medal with similar words inscribed.*

Geraldine: *"Oh, Dear Mother, can this all be happening? Oh, Jesus help me, I praise and thank You. Oh, Mother in Heaven, why,* I didn't ask for it."* (Now my two-year-old son comes up to me and kisses me.)

Holy Mother: **"Be more united to Our Two Hearts and there you will draw all the necessary strength to help you to do My Son's Will."**

214.

Be kind

12 May 1994 *Thursday* *Ascension of the Lord Solemnity*

Holy Mother:

"Dear daughter, in spite of your sins, I still love you. Do not be discouraged, all will be well. Be kind and loving and I will bless you for this."

215.

Do not abandon your faith

12 May 1994 *Thursday* *Ascension of the Lord Solemnity*

Holy Mother:

Message for ....

"Write down what I say, it is important. My son, do not fear, I am with you. My son, I have prayed to the Father unceasingly for your intentions, so whatever the outcome, try to be at peace and accept God's will in your life. I know, My child, your sorrow, and I weep with you. But the Divine hand of My Son is about to come upon the whole world in justice, for the purification of the world, so offer all

---

* *When I asked Holy Mother, why me?, and my son came over to kiss me, I felt Jesus was using him to show me He gives this to me because He loves me.*

to Me, your Heavenly Mother. I shall assist you and be close to you always. Do not abandon your faith, My child, God is with you, and do not despair, for the grace of God will sustain you. I love you, My son, and I bless you in the name of the Father, and of the Son and of the Holy Spirit."

216.

Consecrate yourself to Me

14 May 1994 *Saturday* *Feast of St. Matthias, Apostle*

Holy Mother:

"My daughter, I wish to convey to you the cause of My innermost suffering. Satan is waging war on My children in a very vicious way. You must consecrate yourself to Me and be always mindful of My Motherly protection. My children, the Evil One will deceive you in many ways. Stay close to My maternal heart and Jesus will help you. The world is in a dreadful state of sin. The battle is worsening, arm yourself with the Holy Rosary and receive the Sacrament of Holy Communion."

217.

Beloved, come embrace Me

19 May 1994 *Thursday 9.00 am*

At Adoration on Retreat

I am at present in front of Jesus in Blessed Sacrament, in adoration and I am happy just to pray and love Them (i. e. Jesus and His Blessed Mother), when Holy Mother suddenly and unexpectedly appears. I only see Her face. She is so beautiful, so, so beautiful, She has a veil covering Her head. I do not want to stop looking at Her. How beautiful a Mother we have in Heaven! Praise You Jesus, and thank You for this precious gift.

Holy Mother:

"My child, take your pen and write. Continue, My child (I did not want to open my eyes in case She would go). **Thank you, My daughter, for coming, I have prepared this grace for you. This is My gift to you from Jesus, My Son. He is pleased to see you happy and content and to come closer to Our Two Hearts. My child, how My Immaculate Heart rejoices in you. My child, the love I have for you is so great. Be always in My heart. I will always be here for you, to sustain you. Daughter, I am delighted to announce to you that My Son is preparing something special for you."**

Geraldine: *"Holy Mother, I don't understand?"*

Holy Mother: **"Daughter, when the time comes, you will know what I mean. Rejoice in Our Love and delight in this hour in which God is giving your soul great graces.**

Tell .... My heart rejoices in her love for Me. I have blessed her abundantly and given her great gifts. Be always close to her as My heart is in her and I delight in her soul.

Permit Me, daughter, to take you on a journey with Me. Come rest in Me and I will delight your soul and lift it to new heights. Be at peace, I will guide you. Come, My child, I am here, come to prepare your heart to receive My Son. My child, do you remember when My son .... said to spend one hour in adoration with Jesus each day? Well if you can't make it, then say ten Our Fathers, ten Hail Marys and ten Glory Be's. This will suffice. Daughter, the journey I wish to take you on is eternal, be at peace, I give you My love. Finish for now."

I felt so much love coming from Our Lady, I was crying with joy. So much joy I felt my heart would burst with joy, Her love is so, so wonderful. I felt Our Lady's love for me and I nearly died of joy. This one experience, I feel, will take me through all the sufferings of my life. Jesus told me, weeks ago, that I would go on this retreat and it was a grace from Him and later in the year, He will fulfil my desires (special prayer requests) as a wonderful gift of His Love. (These were subsequently granted.)

218.

Message for children

23 May 1994 *Monday 4.15 pm*

Holy Mother to little children:

"My dear little children, it is I, your Holy Mother. My little children, I want to tell you to listen to and love your mother and father, in doing so you please God greatly. I, My little children, am with you always, make Me happy by praying a little every day as a family. Weep with Me for the sins in the world which crucify My Son every day. He died and suffered to save you, do not make Him suffer any more. I ask you, My little children, to love Me and My Son more. Offer all your pains to Me and My Son and I will bless you greatly and I will take you all to Paradise to receive your reward that will last forever. Pray and talk to Me often, go to Mass and serve God with a pure heart, making up for all He suffers. I love you and do not want your condemnation. Satan wishes to take your souls, stay close to Me and I will protect you and your family from the Evil One. Go in peace. I bless you in the name of the Father and of the Son and of the Holy Spirit."

219.

Proclaim My Son to this sinful world

25 May 1994 *Wednesday* *St. Bede the Venerable*
St. Gregory VII, Pope
St. Mary Magdalene de Pazzi
Optional Memorials

Holy Mother:

"Daughter, I will pray for your meeting on Friday. Be yourself, do not worry, speak as if it were My Son to whom you are speaking. Pray, and the Holy Spirit will guide and enlighten you. I, My daughter, bless you and I pray to Jesus to give you courage, peace and humility. You, My daughter, are chosen to proclaim My Son to this sinful world.

Tell of the need, because of our sinful nature, for people to be reminded often of what God desires (that is why the messages seem to repeat themselves), **and make known how God wants unity, prayer, love and suffering to appease His anger. I will help you and be with you holding your hand. The Angels and Saints rejoice in you and will assist you, pray and let God's will be done. Praise be to Jesus, true God and true Man. Go in peace."**

220.

Accept My gifts

28 May 1994 *Saturday*

My dream of my Mum coming to Australia came true. Jesus gave me two graces, He said she would come: the Retreat and Mum. And there is more to come.

Holy Mother:

Yesterday She said, **"Write to .... immediately, he is suffering very much and I wish to use you to help him."**

Today my child is sick and I did not receive Holy Communion. Because of this I feel I have no strength or energy. I feel so terrible when I don't receive Jesus, I feel this way, like I am dying. When I receive Him, He is my strength and joy. Now I cannot survive without Him daily.

221.

I have called you to holiness

28 May 1994 *Saturday 12.15 am*

Holy Mother:

"Daughter, tell My children not to be afraid. I am, My children, close to you. Pray a great deal and you will feel My presence more. I have not forsaken you, Satan's time is very short now. Offer yourselves as victim souls in repa-

ration so that the sufferings accompanying the purification may be lessened. Children of the world, be united to your Heavenly Mother in difficult times and I will give you supernatural strength to sustain you. God is with you in suffering, unite your wounds to His. Children of this depraved humanity, how many times I have called you to holiness, but only a few listen. Behold My Son, who alone is the light of this world, He will guide you to eternity. I am praying unceasingly for you to survive the remaining time of purification*. Trust in Me and do not despair, offer all to Me and I will help you more to come closer to Jesus. You are My precious children whom I will never abandon. Pray, pray, pray."

222.
Love suffering

28 May 1994 *Saturday*

Holy Mother:

"My child, time is of the essence. Too much time has been wasted. Let whoever will do the messages the quickest do them, but be at peace with everyone.

Child, do not worry, I hold you in My Immaculate Heart. Only in Me will you find the peace you so desire. I take the greatest delight in your love for Me. (Here I smell roses. I feel Her love. It is wonderful!) **Love suffering. Offer all and be at peace. Satan is furious with you, but the grace of God will sustain you throughout. Satan will lose, as We are much stronger. Do not fear. Call on My Saints to help and pray for you."**

I felt Them so close to me, like friends. I felt so much love, I cried with joy. I felt Her love for me and I knew I had nothing to fear. Then when I had to go, I did not want to leave Her all alone in the church. (I was praying at Her statue and there was no one else in the church.)

---

* *"Purification": a time of suffering (a suffering partially, at least, brought about by the many sins of people) through which humankind is brought back to its senses and to a sincere return to God.*

223.

Save souls

29 May 1994 *Sunday* *Solemnity of the Holy Trinity*

Holy Mother:

"Dear child, I hear your prayer.* **It is I, your Holy Mother. Write down what I say:**

The next volume is to be started immediately as the next publication is to be in the next year, 1995. My child, tell Father what I am saying to you, it is very important. The date is to coincide with the last feast day in February. Daughter, the time is crucial, you must act immediately. (Holy Mother sounds firm on this.) **Be vigilant, My daughter, in everything. Do as Father tells you and be not afraid, I am assisting you in this endeavour. Remember that My love is always there to sustain you, and remember the joy in Heaven over one sinner saved is immense, so save souls by your prompt response to My pleas.**

I bless you abundantly as does My Son, in the name of the Father, and of the Son, and of the Holy Spirit."

224.

Pray many hearts are opened

3 June 1994 *First Friday* *Sts. Charles Lwanga and Companions, Memorial*

Holy Mother:

"My child, be at peace, God is guiding everything. Do not worry or be concerned. I will permit whatever happens. I wish you to give the messages to .... because this is another door which My Son has opened for you. Pray, many hearts will be touched and opened. Praise and thank My Divine Son for such favours in which you have been allowed to participate. I bless you in the name of the Father, and of the Son, and of the Holy Spirit."

* *Geraldine prayed to Our Lady for a message for a person in difficulty.*

225.

Trust yourself to Me

3 June 1994 *First Friday, Sts. Charles Lwanga and Companions Memorial*

Holy Mother:

"Dear child, I hear your prayer.* It is I, your Holy Mother. Write down what I say:

Oh, My dearest son .... how I long to console you. Do not be afraid, I am with you as we speak. My Son Jesus, My Divine Son will light the way for you. Trust yourself to Me completely for I am guiding your every step. My son, soon you will be blessed with a great grace. Praise and thank the Lord continuously. I have called you here to help Me in my plan of Salvation for the world. Your suffering is precious to Me. When you offer it to Me, I bestow an abundance of graces on you. I promise you, My son, I will never abandon you to your enemies even though it may seem so for a while. I am with you close to your heart and beside you in everything. Go forward in peace and confidence, and wait for My Son to act as He surely will soon. Be courageous, My son. I give you My special blessing and I will give you the grace to endure everything for Me. Go in peace."**

226.

Have your home blessed

8 June 1994 *Wednesday*

Holy Mother:

To My son ....

"My son, do not despair, all will be well. I wish you to have your home blessed and have an Enthronement to My Son done in it. Say the prayer of Family Consecration

* *Geraldine prayed to Our Lady for a message for a person in difficulty.*

** *Here – another part of the world.*

daily for protection. My son, I am with you, helping and assisting you. Be not afraid, the Evil One cannot harm you. I am, My son, preparing you for more trials. However, do not be sad, I will give you special graces to endure. Offer it all to Me and I will help you to rise above this. Be calm and of good cheer in spite of your suffering. I will help you to cope better, pray more, and trust in Me to sustain you, My son. Go in peace. I love you."

227.

The Sign of the Cross

12 June 1994 *Eleventh Sunday of the Year*

Holy Mother:

Holy Mother always asks me to bless myself before a message, as the Evil One flees when we make the Sign of the Cross.

228.

Live My messages

12 June 1994 *Sunday 3.00 pm*

Holy Mother:

"My daughter, I, your Holy Mother, love you with a great love. I am preparing you for the Coming of My Son, listen to My voice when I call as I love you and wish you to be close to Me and My Son. I rejoice in your motherhood and I wish you to confide to Me the secrets of your heart and I will console you in your difficulties, do not worry or be concerned about this matter, the Lord will provide abundantly. Trust, pray and live My messages and the rest will be given in abundance. You are a great joy to My heart and I welcome your love with open arms as does My Son too. Go in peace."

229.

I desire a medal to be struck

Early June 1994

Holy Mother:

"Daughter, it is I, Holy Mother, please write for souls. My child, you must tell Father I desire and My Divine Son, Jesus also requires, the messages regarding the medal to be placed at the front of the book in an appropriate place, all this on one page. My child, My beloved Son, Jesus and I desire a medal to be struck. I wish this medal to be spread far and wide as this is the Medal of Divine Mercy and of devotion to Our Two Hearts. Let all who spread devotion to Our Two Hearts and Divine Mercy be assured of a great place in Heaven, as these devotions rekindled will be the onset to the Triumph of My Immaculate Heart, which My Son desires greatly. Pray much for this intention and for these last days preceding the Triumph of My Immaculate Heart.

My beloved child, may the greatest blessing of Almighty God be upon all who do as I ask. Go in peace."

This is the description which Our Lady gave of the medal:

The front of medal:

The Two Hearts
with the inscription

"The Immaculate
Conception
and the Sacred Heart
of Jesus unite the World"

The back of medal:

Jesus of Mercy
with the inscription

"Jesus
the Light of the World.
He who believes in Me
will never die."

Our Lady:

"I will personally bless* anyone who wears this medal, it is a sign of My love."

230.

Mother of the World, Consoler of Hearts

14 June 1994 *Tuesday*

Someone had asked me under what title had Our Lady appeared to me. So I prayed about this.

Holy Mother:

"I have appeared to you under the title of:

**'MOTHER OF THE WORLD,
CONSOLER OF HEARTS'.**

I have come to give you My peace and love and to bring My children closer to Our Two Hearts."

231.

Take time to share with Me

14 June 1994 *Tuesday 11.15 pm*

Holy Mother:

"My beloved child, I am happy that you have taken the time to share your sorrows with Me. I was concerned about you. Do you see how good Jesus is? He only tests you so much and gives you what you need to endure. Thank and praise Him for His goodness. Daughter, I have a message for the Prayer Group and My children in general."

---

* *As a mother can bless and invoke God's blessing on her children, but of course Our Lady's blessing would be exceptional and much more powerful.*

232.

Make "Love" your constant goal

14 June 1994

Holy Mother:

"My dear beloved children, your Holy Mother blesses you one and all. I have come to thank each and every one of you for consoling and persevering with Me and My Divine Son, Jesus. Our Hearts are rejoicing in your Cenacles and Heaven rejoices in them too. The grace of God will always be bestowed upon all those present at these Cenacles. I wish to tell you of My suffering and remind you of how My heart is pierced daily by the wickedness of those children who do not wish to know Me, so I come to you, My devoted little ones: My heart, which is wounded beyond belief, pleads with you, and I offer you also His Chalice from which to drink (the chalice of suffering and sacrifice). **Daily I suffer greatly as does My Son. So I share with you My heart full of sorrow and anguish and I desire that together we console one another and share our suffering together. Forgive one another all offences and live as My holy children, modelled and fashioned after Me. I desire that you lift one another up and support each other in suffering. Be Jesus for each other and I will bless you for this. I am preparing you for My Son's Return. So make it your constant goal to live in love, disarming My Adversary, who, on account of souls you bring to Me, hates you. Be always in prayer and I will always be close to love, protect and defend you. My beloved little children, I thank you and I bless each one of you from My heart. Go in peace."**

233.

Read the Scriptures

23 June 1994 *Thursday*

Jesus:

"Daughter, I want you to read the Scriptures every day and live it. This is My gift to you."

234.

I have not forsaken you

23 June 1994 *Thursday*

Jesus:

"My son, I, Jesus, have not forsaken you. This suffering is for your purification. I am close to you and I give you My promise to sustain you. Be not afraid, I have come to help and console you in your affliction. I am preparing the way, trust in Me, I am guiding everything. Be calm and keep your peace of mind and have recourse to My Mother, who suffers as I speak. Be of good cheer in spite of your troubles, for the grace of God will sustain you. Be at peace and trust in Me, all will be well. I give you My blessing. Go in peace."

235.

You must be holy and prepared

23 June 1994 *Thursday*

God the Father:

"My children, I, God the Father speak to you one and all. Be holy, live holy lives. Be loving and kind, turn the other cheek. Offer to Me your sacrifices. I will reward you in full for your fidelity. Be not afraid, I will avenge the persecutors of My innocent children. Hold on a little longer,* I am preparing a very great punishment. You must be holy

* *I. e. persevere, even though you are suffering.*

and prepared. Suffer for love of Me and share My sorrow and grief (like the grief of the father in the parable of the Prodigal Son), **and afterwards you will share My Kingdom for all eternity. Be, My children, of one mind, holy and good like Mary, your Mother. I give Her to you. Pray for deliverance, strength and courage to continue to do My will. I am with you always. Be at peace.**

Daughter, I wish you to write, on your knees, because you have been given many graces."

236.

Are you prepared to receive My love?

1 July 1994 *First Friday*

At Adoration

Jesus:

"My daughter, I am happy you have come. It does not matter if you fall a hundred times, as long as you come back to the Sacrament of Reconciliation. I am waiting with open arms to love you and forgive you. The more you come, the more I will bless you. This is how you know God's children from the children of the world. God's children want to be forgiven and do not wish to continue to sin. But the children of the world do not want forgiveness. Daughter, I want to ask everyone a question." He asked me first. **"Are you prepared to receive My love?"*** I find myself looking into my life wondering what I can change to be more prepared, if I have to stand in front of Jesus now. Are we prepared if He comes now? He wants us to examine our consciences to see what we need to correct in our lives. Then He said, **"I want you to change your faults."** I understood this to mean we must try to overcome our bad habits or faults, as they will have grave

* *I. e. "To receive the fulness of My love in Heaven" – meaning "Are you prepared for Heaven now?" Or, in other words, "Are you ready at any moment to leave this life?" He says this because He wants us to be prepared for Him when He comes to take us, so that we can go directly to Heaven as He does not want us to suffer in Purgatory.*

consequences later on (Purgatory). We must now, while we still have time, correct them. Then He said, **"Be kinder to your husbands. They do not ask, but they need a lot of kindness.** (He gave me a man's mother as an example.) **A mother is kind to her children, that is why she is loved so much. In the same way, the kinder you are to your husband the more he will love you."**

Then He said, **"Use this time wisely with your children** (Holidays)**. Talk to them more about Me and My love. Read to them the stories of the Saints, if they still turn away, you have done your duty. But if you do not tell them about Me, know that later on you will have to give Me an account of this** (meaning, if their souls are lost)**."** I understood this to be very serious and important. Then He said, **"I want you to bring the children to Mass every morning. If you do this, I will give you more graces."** He then told me to contact a friend of mine, as we would strengthen one another, and He asked me to go to a particular prayer group where there is Adoration, Mass, Rosary and Novenas. He said He could make it possible for me to go, and I will receive great graces, if I go to this Prayer Group.

237.

I am with you

1 July 1994 *First Friday*

Jesus:

I asked about a particular situation. Jesus said, **"They will persecute you as they did Me, before you. But if they do, let it be for doing good, or for the truth. Let it not be for any wrongdoing. Then hold your head high for I am with you."**

238.

Leave it in My Son's hands

5 July 1994 *Tuesday, St. Anthony Zaccaria Optional Memorial*

Holy Mother:

For ....

"Tell My son not to be afraid, do not worry. Be at peace. All will be well about the past, leave it in My Son's hands. Go forth and proclaim My Son's name." (I understood – do not worry, do God's will.)

239.

Purgatory

10 July 1994 *Fifteenth Sunday of the Year*

Holy Mother:

Today I asked Holy Mother about Purgatory. She said that the souls there have the grace of God to sustain them and the joy of looking forward to the glory of God to strengthen them in their suffering and they are very close to us.

240.

Listen and put into practice what I say

11 July 1994 *Monday* *St. Benedict, Abbot Memorial*

Holy Mother:

"My child, it is I, Holy Mother, I have come to tell you the secrets of My heart. Today I am very sad, I am weeping bitterly over My lost children for whom people forget to pray, I love them dearly. But they will not listen, please console Me in My grief and pray with Me for their

conversion. I am so sorrowful, My grief is beyond words. Daughter, consoler of My heart, be the remedy for My sorrow in these days of confusion and apostasy. I wish My beloved Priests to pray more in their hearts for My intentions. This will console Me greatly. To My faithful children persevering in My Cenacles, know, My beloved ones, My special Motherly Grace will sustain you always. Be of good cheer, in spite of your troubles, it is necessary that you suffer a little, for so much the greater will be your joy later. Look only towards Heaven in your trials. I am beside you, protecting you, guiding and helping you, listen then to what the Lord wishes you to know. My beloved ones, the world is in My* and My beloved Son's hands, so fear nothing, except not doing My Son's will. Listen and put into practice what I say. (What Our Lady says is always in accordance with God's will.) **Go in peace."**

241.

It fills My heart with great joy when you desire to console Me

July 1994

After Prayer of Reparation

Jesus:

"Daughter, I wish to tell all My children of My great love for them. How many times I have desired to embrace each one of you, I am so happy that you desire to console Me. It will be your greatest joy in Heaven. My children, the time is coming when you will see Me in all My glory, pray for this day. I wait with great excitement. Accept My gift of love to you to help you to continue on your journey to Me. I am rejoicing in your love for Me. It fills My heart with great joy when you desire to console Me. I thank you and bless each one of you abundantly. Pray for sinners."

* *Emphasizes Our Lady's power and influence over everything because of Her unique relationship with Her Son. Ultimately, of course everything is totally in God's hands.*

242.

Be spiritually strong

July 1994

Holy Mother:

"There will come a time when people will flock to you in despair,* I am preparing you for this time, you must be spiritually strong."

243.

I accept you and your weaknesses

21 July 1994 *Thursday* *St. Lawrence of Brindisi Optional Memorial*

Holy Mother:

"Dear daughter, please do not be sad, I love you just as you are. I accept you and your weaknesses, don't despair, I am helping you to help others. Do not worry, My grace will be with you always to do My Son's will. I will not abandon you, offer your distress for conversion of sinners."

Geraldine: *"Holy Mother, please forgive me, I love You with all my heart. Please forgive me I am so useless without You and Jesus."*

Holy Mother: **"My dearest daughter, your tears are a joy to Me, be at peace and feel My love and joy. I, too, love you immensely. Never fear. Daughter, My heart is still grieving over My lost children, pray more for their conversion and ask others to do the same. Remind My children** of My constant presence among them. You are My dearest, dearest children so faithful to My Son, you are enfolded in My Immaculate Heart. Comfort each other always, and be good**

---

* *There will come a time when things will be so bad in the world and people will be so discouraged that they will seek spiritual comfort.*

** *Referring to groups of people who pray together regularly – reciting the Rosary and other prayers.*

to each other as Jesus, My Son, is to you. My beloved child, pray to Sr. Faustina, she will help you to continue your mission. The cut-off date for the book is the last feast day in the month of August 1994."

244.

Spread devotion to Me everywhere

24 July 1994 *Seventeenth Sunday of the Year*

The Divine Infant Jesus:

"My dear daughter, it is I, the Infant Jesus. I have come in this way to teach you to be a small child, pure and innocent, trusting in the arms of its mother. I am close to you and wish to share with you My suffering, as many young children are senselessly murdered each day. Heaven itself is horrified at this wicked generation. My Father can take no more, His wrath is about to fall on this world. I come as a child to plead with you for this wicked humanity. Say the prayers of the Infant Jesus of Prague and promote devotion to Me everywhere. I wish you to console My Mother in this way, as I will take all the suffering children into My heart. I bless you and love you. Be at peace. Go, spread My messages everywhere." *

245.

Pray more in silence and obscurity

24 July 1994 *Seventeenth Sunday of the Year*

Jesus:

"Daughter, it is Jesus, write down what I say. Daughter, I love you, be at peace. Rest in Me and I will lift you up, consider My suffering and unite yours to Mine, I am

* *See message No. 247 (or Appendix A), and Appendix C for prayers to the Infant Jesus of Prague.*

eternal, abide in Me, I am all love. Daughter, I will send you more suffering, but I will give you more graces to endure. Offer all to Me for the purification of the world. My daughter, I am preparing you through My messages to do My Holy Will. Use the time available to you to do My Holy Will. Be of good cheer and know I assist you in your daily duty, I am at present helping you to overcome yourself at this time. I wish you to pray more in silence and obscurity and continue to fulfil My desires by continuing to do the work I have entrusted to you. My Adversary is trying to stop all My plans concerning this mission; continue to write in spite of his deceitfulness and obstructions, and My Holy Mother will assist you in this endeavour. I bless you, go in peace."

246.

Accept all as coming from Me

24 July 1994 *Seventeenth Sunday of the Year*

Jesus:

"Daughter, tell My son this dream means I am soon bringing him to a new spiritual awareness. Tell him I am pleased and happy with his efforts and it delights My heart when he honours Me. Do not be worried or disturbed about anything, I am with you, guiding everything, accept all as coming from Me. Go in peace."

247.

Prayer to the Infant Jesus by Holy Mother

28 July 1994 *Thursday*

"Offer Your Lives For The Salvation Of Souls.

I pray You, Dear Infant Jesus,
to accept all the suffering children

of the world and those in Purgatory
into Your most tender and loving Heart.
Be for them the refuge and
consolation they so desire.
I pray and offer all I do
every day of my life for their salvation.
Amen."

Holy Mother:

"Dear child, this prayer I give you will be for the comfort and salvation of many suffering children. Said daily, this will obtain many graces."

248.

Fast, do penance and sacrifice yourselves

30 July 1994 *Saturday 11.00 pm* *St. Peter Chrysologus Optional Memorial*

Holy Mother:

"My child, I desire from My children complete fidelity to My Immaculate Heart. Pray more for My suffering children. Fast, do penance and sacrifice yourselves and My Son will repay you greatly. Be on your guard against those who cause divisions. Be careful with your words, as you will suffer for them later. Judge no one lest you be judged yourself. I wish you to remain calm in all afflictions, offering everything to Me and My Divine Son, Jesus. Be always close to Me, constantly thinking of My desires and how you can help Me. Comfort Me often and pray more from your heart. Heaven, My children, is watching as you do the will of My Son. So be always aware of Our presence in your lives. I bless you from My heart."

249.

Dedicate the work to the Holy Family

30 July 1994 *Saturday 11.00 pm* *St. Peter Chrysologus Optional Memorial*

Holy Mother:

"Yes, My child, I am pleased with the efforts you are all making. Tell .... I am happy he is guiding and correcting you. I rejoice in your working together, as you, My child, have much to learn and I am happy My sons are cooperating with each other and are united in this work. This gives My heart great joy. I wish all My sons (i. e. Priest sons) **to be closer, so they can support one another in trials and difficulties, and encourage one another. In this way grace flows from My heart to theirs** (i. e. Our Lady is more able to obtain graces for them from God and in this way grace flows from Her heart to theirs). **Continue to do the work My Son has entrusted to you. Many souls will rejoice in these messages and many will be comforted and consoled, knowing our desires. This work will bear much good fruit. Dedicate it to the Holy Family, as most of the messages encourage holiness in families. I bless all your undertakings. Go in peace to love and serve the Lord."**

250.

If I withdraw, it's only to bring you closer through prayer

3 August 1994 *Wednesday*

At Adoration

Jesus:

For a day or two now it seems like Jesus has withdrawn from me, yet I don't know why. I cannot begin to say how that feels. I feel so alone, lost, afraid and wondering what I have done

and if Jesus will find someone else. My soul is in agony. The loss of His presence is more than I can bear. I would die a thousand horrible deaths rather than be without Him. This agony seemed like an eternity to me. Then I was tormented by doubts. It seemed I was imagining everything. Then I went to Mass, Adoration and Rosary and two Novenas. During Adoration, Jesus made His presence known to me. I felt my whole being enveloped in this great love. As He spoke, He assured me of His great love for me and told me, **"If I withdraw, it's only to bring you closer to Me through prayer. Only other people's prayers are sustaining you and on account of the messages you are in great danger."** (I understood that Satan will redouble his efforts to stop me.) Then Jesus said, **"Your prayers must be persevering, fervent and trusting to withstand everything."** He assured me, all will be well regarding worries I had over other things. Then He said, **"Because I love you, I wish to share My suffering. Will you share in My suffering?"** I said, *"Yes,"* but I did not fully understand how. But I felt it was a great privilege He was giving me. Afterwards and the next day my suffering was great, very great – not physical, but as if my heart was pierced by a great hurt. At Mass the next day I offered all through my tears. Again, I understand the great value suffering has in Jesus' eyes. It is a beautiful gift that unites us more to Him. On the way to adoration Wednesday night, Holy Mother spoke too, confirming all this. She reassured me that Jesus loved me and She also spoke to me about praying more. Then She said to tell .... all She has said regarding this. When I felt Jesus' love I cried in joy, like a bride united to her loved one. Then all doubts and fears left me. Then Jesus said, **"Tell all My children I am with each one of them."** (I felt this within every part of me. He is very much with us and I felt full of joy, hope and love for each of us. Blessed be God!)

251.

Learn to venerate Me more

3 August 1994 *Wednesday*

Holy Mother:

As I am taking a message sitting: **"My child, you must learn to venerate Me more. My daughter, I have a message for Father and the Group. Be at peace, Father will discern.**

My son, I bless you from My heart's flame of love. My son, I desire that all My children come and venerate Me on My birthday, giving God great praise, thanks and adoration for this blessed occasion which God has given. I will be present among you delighting in this as I wish to give praise and thanks to My Son Jesus through My children. Behold your Mother in prayer on this blessed day and rejoice with all the Angels and Saints in Heaven, giving honour, praise and glory to God. Thank you, My beloved son."

252.

Be faithful and persevering to the end

3 August 1994 *Wednesday*

Holy Mother:

"Daughter, tell all My children I am delighted they came in such great numbers. I will remind you always of My presence among you. Be faithful and persevering to the end, constantly striving for goodness in everything. Be loving, faithful children with a will to console their God. Go in peace."

253.

Behold My broken body and say the Chaplet of Divine Mercy

5 August 1994 First Friday 8.00 pm Dedication of St. Mary Major Optional Memorial

Adoration

Jesus:

Tonight I see Jesus crucified on the Cross, He was in the most pitiful state. Blood was pouring down His face, arms, hands and body so much, I could see the agony on His face as He looked up towards Heaven, I cried so much to see Him suffering like this. Now, my suffering is nothing compared to what He is suffering, and I feel like praying continuously to console Him. If only everyone could see Him this way they would never stop praying. Jesus says, **"Behold My Broken Body, and say the Chaplet of Divine Mercy."** I ask Our Lord why doesn't He let others see Him like this, so they can console Him. He says, **"My sheep know My voice, he who believes and has not seen is blessed."** Then He tells me I must not wound Him more by speaking of my suffering as I would lose graces.

254.

Come full of hope and confidence

9 August 1994 Tuesday

Holy Mother:

"My child, I wish to speak to you about Perfection. You will never reach perfection on earth, there will always be something you are not happy about. So you come as a child to My Son Jesus, trusting in His Divine Mercy. I ask only that you keep trying to do the best you can and come full of hope and confidence."

255.

Ask for graces

9 August 1994 *Tuesday 11.00 pm*

Sr. Faustina told me she wished me to tell everyone that God has given her special graces to bestow on all who pray to her, so she wants us to ask for these graces and she said, **"Do not be afraid of suffering, if you were to die a million deaths of terrible torture, it could never compare to the great delights God has prepared for us in Heaven."** She said that the more I suffer the more Jesus will delight my heart and to be at peace. She is praying for me. I feel she is a sister to me.

256.

Offer adoration and Mass

13 August 1994 *Saturday* *St. Pontian, Pope and St. Hippolytus Optional Memorial*

Holy Mother:

"Your meeting with .... will go well, but offer Adoration and Mass for this too. Tell .... all I have said and that We wish you to pray more."

(This meeting, which was of great importance, went very well.)

257.

Many will perish

13 August 1994 *Saturday* *St. Pontian, Pope and St. Hippolytus Optional Memorial*

Jesus:

"My beloved, it is I, Jesus. Beloved of My heart, I desire that you become completely united to Me. Come into My heart and we will be united as one, come to Me in the Blessed Sacrament. Why do you avoid Me? I wish to open My Divine Heart burning with great love. My desire is to envelope you in the fire of My heart's love and we will be united in love. My love is overflowing. Thank you, My daughter, for taking time to be with Me. This work is so vital for the salvation of many souls. I wish to share with you My agony. My sorrow is immense. I desire that all My children be saved. I am so grieved at the wickedness of this world. Help Me to bring My children back to God. Time is so short. Many will perish unless generous souls make sacrifices and pray in reparation, as the just anger of My Father must be appeased. This book will come out at a time when many will be in great despair.

I wish a prayer to be written at the beginning of the book, so all who read it will receive the graces contained therein. Pray for open hearts to receive this grace to come closer to My and My Holy Mother's heart. Only there will they find the consolation they seek."

258.

I will protect your home

13 August 1994 *Saturday* *St. Pontian, Pope and St. Hippolytus Optional Memorial*

Infant Jesus:

I came across a statue of the Infant Jesus in a jumble sale. I bought it and took it home and I was going to give it away as a present as it is very beautiful. Then the Infant Jesus said, **"I came to you to be with you, if you leave Me here I will protect your home. Put Me in a place of veneration."**

259.

My Son's happiness is Mine

19 August 1994 *Friday* *St. John Eudes Optional Memorial*

I ask about someone's birthday.

Holy Mother:

"It is My desire that .... be given first preference in this matter, because My Son's happiness is Mine. In this I rejoice."

260.

Come taste the delights of My heart

19 August 1994 *Sunday*

At a House of Religious

Jesus:

(I had just become a Novice in a Third Order of Religious.)

"My beloved, now we are one, the floodgates of My heart are open to you, come abide in Me. (Here I feel Jesus' love.) **You are Mine, come taste the delights of My**

heart. Do not worry about anything, it is just you and I together." Here I feel one with Jesus and I do not worry about anyone, only that I am absorbed in Jesus. The night before He was speaking to me all night in and out of my sleep. I was aware of Him speaking words of great love and my heart was full of delight and excitement.

I dearly wanted a cross as a souvenir on the day I became a Novice (Tertiary), and I asked Jesus if He could make it possible for me to purchase one from the Religious House. He said, **"It will not be possible, Daughter, I will give you the greatest cross of all, My cross!"**

261.

I will help you in all your difficulties

22 August 1994 *Monday* *Feast of the Queenship of Mary*

Holy Mother:

At the prayer group, I hear Holy Mother say:

"My child, I am present. (I see Her bless each one of us individually with the Sign of the Cross on our foreheads.) **Tell My children, I bless each one abundantly for coming here today to pray. Tell them Jesus, My Divine Son, will help them in all their difficulties."**

262.

Pray for virtues

23 August 1994 *Tuesday* *St. Rose of Lima Optional Memorial*

Holy Mother:

This morning after Holy Communion, I asked Holy Mother in prayer about virtues, and to help me to love more with Her peace and love. Holy Mother said, **"Only through prayer**

and a desire for these virtues will they develop in you." At that moment I saw Holy Mother standing over me, I was kneeling with Her hand on my head and She said, **"I give you My love, My peace, go give it to everyone."** After this all day I am filled with great love for everyone, I was bursting with so much love. It was glorious, I felt God's presence in me so much, I felt I will die of joy.

I asked Jesus if I should visit ...., and because Jesus said He was happy about this, I also felt He would be happy if I took that person Holy Communion at the same time, as I am a special minister of the Eucharist. The Parish Priest approved of me doing this, so I went.

263.

Come back and all will be forgiven

24 August 1994 *Wednesday* *Feast of St. Bartholomew, Apostle*

Jesus:

"Daughter, My beloved, it is I, Jesus. I wish a prayer to be put at the beginning of the book (the prayer below). **This book is to be dedicated to the Holy Family:**

> **'Father, bless all who read this book and may all hearts be opened to receive the graces contained therein. I ask this in the name of Jesus, through the intercession of Mary and St. Joseph.**
>
> **Amen.'**

I, Jesus, desire all My children to spread devotion to My Sacred Heart. Let My children know that I long to give them My love. I want no one to be afraid to come. I desire all to be forgiven, for I died that you all may have life. Come, My children, come back and all will be forgiven. My Sacred Heart burns with love for you. Choose Paradise, where you will partake in what I have prepared for you for all eternity. Choose life, not death. Come and I will fill you with good things. Your heart will be restless till it rests in Me. I bless

you and Love blesses you." (Here I feel Jesus' great longing for us to return to Him – I feel the anguish of His heart; His heart is breaking in His desire that we return to Him no matter what we have done. I feel this more in this, than in any other message. This is the main message in which Jesus makes known how He longs with all His heart for our return, no matter how far we have strayed.)

264.

Rejoice, for Heaven and earth are united in these times

24 August 1994 *Wednesday* *Feast of St. Bartholomew, Apostle*

Jesus:

"Daughter, I wish to tell you of My great joy. Daughter, My heart rejoices in this mission. My love will transform you and bring you to life everlasting. Daughter, know that Heaven is rejoicing in this work. Daughter, continue on regardless of the struggles you may face. Daughter, come rest in My heart and let Me set you on fire. Daughter, rejoice, for Heaven and earth are united in these times. Daughter, rejoice, for I am coming soon to give you your reward." I felt the happiness of Jesus as He rejoiced in the souls that would come to Him through this work.

265.

Continue to adore and love your God

26 August 1994 *Friday*

At Adoration

Jesus:

"Tell My children to continue to love Me and uphold My teaching."

Geraldine: *"Lord, do I offend You, writing now (during adoration)?"*

Jesus: **"Daughter, when you do My will, how can you offend Me? Daughter, the Saints are beside you, behold your brothers and sisters** (the Saints)**, share in their blessedness."**

During Mass

Jesus:

"Hold up My children to Me, offer this Mass for unbelievers."

Holy Mother:

"Thank you, My child, for being faithful to our call. Tell My children, the heart of My Son is offended beyond belief. Console Jesus. Enough! Rest for now."

Jesus:

"Beloved, come into My heart. You are My Divine * Spouse, ** My Divine * Bride, ** in you I will take My repose. Beloved, take My Cross (daily crosses) **and share My suffering, united we are one. My daughter, have recourse to Me in everything, abide in Me always, do not fear anyone. My power is with you. Beloved, I offer My heart greatly offended by insults, continue to adore and love your God."**

After Holy Communion

Jesus:

"Behold the Lamb of God who takes away the sins of the world! Eat of Me, abide in Me, love Me, adore Me, desire Me, console Me, be with Me, long for Me."

---

* *Divine (twice): In the sense that we, as adopted children, share in God's life, i. e. in the Divine Life, also used perhaps in the sense "precious" or "very dear".*

** *Spouse, Bride: Jesus is the Bridegroom, the Church is His Bride. Each of us as a member of the Church have Jesus as the Divine Bridegroom.*

During Rosary after Mass

Holy Mother:

"Daughter, I am present, thank you for consoling My Son." She kisses* me on my cheeks with great joy and says, **"The Grace of God is upon all those in the church."**

This message sums up many of the things that Jesus and Mary are asking:

The Mother of God speaks

5 October 1994

"My Son desires that you listen and obey all that I ask:

I ask for prayers for the opening of hearts to accept consecration to My Immaculate Heart.

I ask for prayers for an outpouring of the Holy Spirit in all countries, especially Russia.

I ask for devotion to Our Two Hearts in this age.

I ask for prayers for all those consecrated to My Immaculate Heart to continue to remain therein.

I ask special prayers for all those Clergy experiencing difficulty in following the Vicar of Christ on earth.

I ask for prayers for all the Faithful that they may remain close to God in all trials.

I ask for global unity in these dark times which have come upon you."

---

* *Holy Mother kissed me as She was so happy we had consoled Jesus and Herself through our prayer. If we only knew the value of prayer and how happy it makes Them, we would pray much more.*

Appendices

A

Prayer to the Infant Jesus

B

Prayer for Priests

C

Prayer to the Infant Jesus of Prague

D

Prayer to Saint Joseph

E

Prayer for Poor Souls

F

Prayer for the Cause of Life

G

Visit of Geraldine and her Spiritual Director to her Bishop

H

Distribution Centres

Appendix

A

Prayer to the Infant Jesus

by Holy Mother

"Offer your lives for the salvation of souls."

**"I pray You, dear Infant Jesus,
to accept all the suffering children
of the world and those beyond*
into Your most tender and loving Heart.
Be for them the refuge and
consolation they so desire.
I pray and offer all I do
every day of my life for their salvation."**

Amen

"Dear child, this prayer I give you will be for the comfort and salvation of many suffering children in the world. Said daily, this will obtain many graces."

***SD This must refer to the Children in Purgatory?**

Appendix

B

Prayer for Priests

O my Jesus, I beg You on behalf of the whole Church,
grant it love and the light of Your Spirit
and give power to the words of Priests
so that hardened hearts might be brought to repentance
and return to You, O Lord.
Lord, give us holy Priests,
You Yourself maintain them in holiness.
O Divine and great High Priest,
may the power of Your mercy accompany them
everywhere and protect them
from the devil's traps and snares,
which are continually being set for the souls of Priests.
May the power of Your mercy, O Lord,
shatter and bring to naught all that might tarnish
the sanctity of Priests, for You can do all things.

from the Spiritual Diary of Blessed Sister Faustina

Appendix

C

Prayer to the Infant Jesus of Prague

O humble Infant of Prague,
my Lord and my God.
Protector of the land of my birth,
Source of unity and strength.
Morning Star and Dawn
that gives light to my soul,
illuminate my soul
with the fire of Your love.
Keep me in Your shadow
with the tender love of Your Mother.

Now and always.
Amen.

Imprimatur: Ján Sokol
17th October, 1992
Archbishop of Trnava
Metropolitan of Slovakia

Appendix

D

16 August 1996

Holy Mother:

Prayer to Saint Joseph

O Beloved Saint Joseph, Patron of the Holy Family,
I entrust to you my family,
my life, and the whole human race.
O beautiful Saint Joseph,
how powerful your intercession
before the Throne of God.
May we always, at each and every moment,
entrust ourselves to you,
and may you be our constant source
of inspiration and consolation
in everything we do.

Amen.

Appendix

E

Prayer for Poor Souls

Our Lord told Saint Gertrude that the following prayer would release a vast number of souls each time it is said:

**"Eternal Father, I offer Thee the most precious
Blood of Thy Divine Son, Jesus,
in union with all the Masses being said this day
throughout the world for all the Holy Souls in Purgatory,
for sinners everywhere,
for sinners in the Universal Church,
those in my own home and within my family.**

Amen.

*Approval of His Eminence the Cardinal Patriarch of Lisbon
4 March 1936*

Appendix

F

(Prayer for the Cause of Life)

O Mary,
bright dawn of the new world,
Mother of the living,
to you do we entrust the cause of life:
Look down O Mother,
upon the vast numbers
of babies not allowed to be born,
of the poor whose lives are made difficult,
of men and women
who are victims of brutal violence,
of the elderly and the sick killed,
by indifference or out of misguided mercy.
Grant that all who believe in your Son
may proclaim the Gospel of life
with honesty and love
to the people of our time.
Obtain for them the grace
to accept that Gospel
as a gift ever new,
the joy of celebrating it with gratitude
throughout their lives
and the courage to bear witness to it
resolutely in order to build,
together with all people of good will,
the civilization of truth and love,
to the praise and glory of God,
the Creator and lover of life.

Pope John Paul II

Appendix

G

Distribution Centres*

Website: www.archart.cz/divine-inspirations

SLOVAK REPUBLIC:

Mrs. Elena Lehocká
Eisnerova 15, 841 07 Bratislava, Slovak Republic
Phone: +421-2-64-775-768
E-mail: <mediatrix@stonline.sk>

AUSTRALIA:

Divine Inspirations Distribution Centre
P. O. Box 325, Guildford, New South Wales, 2161
Australia
Phone & fax: 61-2-9688-1097
E-mail: <i_jop@hotkey.net.au>

UNITED STATES OF AMERICA:

Queenship Publishing Company
P. O. Box 220
Goleta, California 93116, U. S. A.
Phone: 1-800-647-9882
Fax: 1 (805) 967-5843
E-mail: <Donna@queenship.org>

* Volume 1 & 2 available in English, other languages will be available in due course; Medal of Divine Mercy available, as well as pamphlet explaining the Medal.

INDEX OF TOPICS

This index is a list of topics taken, for the most part, from the messages themselves. It is meant to be an introduction to the topic that leads one to a more detailed explanation of it. The first number (e. g. 040) is a serial number of the related message, the second number in bold type behind the slant mark (e. g. /**59**) points to the page where this message begins.

I

J

S